GREAT AMERICAN THINKERS

Henry David Thoreau

Writer of the Transcendentalist Movement

Andrew Coddington

Cavendish
Square

New York

Published in 2017 by Cavendish Square Publishing, LLC
243 5th Avenue, Suite 136, New York, NY 10016

Library of Congress Cataloging-in-Publication Data

Names: Coddington, Andrew, author. Title: Henry David Thoreau : writer of the transcendentalist movement /
Andrew Coddington. Description: New York : Cavendish Square Publishing, 2017. | Series: Great American thinkers
| Includes bibliographical references and index. | Description based on print version record and CIP data provided by
publisher; resource not viewed. Identifiers: LCCN 2016001589 (print) | LCCN 2016000634 (ebook) |
ISBN 9781502619297 (ebook) | ISBN 9781502619280 (library bound) Subjects: CSH: Thoreau, Henry David, 1817-1862--Juvenile
literature. | Philosophers--United States--Biography--Juvenile literature. | Transcendentalists (New England)--Biography--Juvenile
literature.Classification: LCC B931.T44 (print) | LCC B931.T44 C63 2016 (ebook) |
DDC 818/.309--dc23
LC record available at http://lccn.loc.gov/2016001589

Editorial Director: David McNamara
Editor: Elizabeth Schmermund
Copy Editor: Rebecca Rohan
Art Director: Jeffrey Talbot
Designer: Amy Greenan
Production Assistant: Karol Szymczuk
Photo Research: J8 Media

Printed in the United States of America

CONTENTS

INTRODUCTION ... 5
Back to Basics

ONE ... 9
Thoreau's Early Life

TWO ... 29
Revealing the Writer

THREE ... 49
Walden

FOUR ... 69
Resistance to Civil Government

FIVE ... 87
Trials and Publications

SIX ... 99
Later Life and Legacy

Chronology / 105

Glossary / 108

Sources / 111

Further Information / 119

Bibliography / 122

Index / 125

About the Author / 128

Back to Basics

Modern life, especially in the United States, is characterized in many ways by extravagance. Access to information is at an all-time high with the ubiquity of the Internet. Smartphones containing endless streams of up-to-the-second statuses and news updates have found a spot in the pockets of most Americans. As a result, the ways in which people work have fundamentally changed, with employees expected to maintain constant communication with their employers at all hours of the day.

American extravagance, however, is not limited to hours worked. Production has exploded as people buy more material goods, including the latest technology and fashions. In order to house more things, Americans buy increasingly larger houses. Today, the average home in the United States is 2,400

Henry David Thoreau's work has always been firmly rooted in the natural world.

square feet (223 square meters), a size that rivals some of the most opulent palaces of the ancient world. Throughout this process of accumulation, Americans have racked up an extraordinary amount of debt. In 2013, the average American household owed nearly one-quarter of a million dollars in credit card, student loan, car loan, and mortgage debt.

This pattern of consumption has recently begun to reveal its flaws. In 2008, the quest for increasing personal profit led many private bankers in charge of risky mortgages to speculate on their value with hardly any oversight. The ploy backfired, causing housing prices to plummet and many people to lose their jobs. Excessive

Unchecked modern consumption has led to many problems, including an explosion in personal debt and severe environmental degradation.

overproduction to furnish an increasingly disposable lifestyle has also harmed our environment, as the world's natural resources are voraciously consumed for products that end up in landfills—or in the ocean. Meanwhile, the demand for cheap energy has grown exponentially over the past several decades. Nonrenewable, unclean energy sources such as coal and petroleum have contributed greatly to climate change, which threatens our world and the future of those who live in it. Many parts of the world, and the United States in particular, have grown addicted to a lifestyle that sacrifices not only the environment and the quality of peoples' lives, but also the belief that an individual is in control of his own destiny.

Given this state of affairs, it is surprising that one of America's most venerated and influential figures is Henry David Thoreau, a Harvard College alumnus who consciously decided to abandon an ordinary life of consumption in the town of Concord, Massachusetts, and take up residence in a one-room cabin on the shores of a small glacial lake called Walden. Yet, in the face of modern excess, there remains a perpetual desire within American society to simplify one's life as Thoreau did and build a cabin in the woods—to pare down one's belongings, to get rid of the technologies that distract one from pursuing one's passions, to purify one's life.

Thoreau's writings from the nineteenth century continue to speak to us today, and they still prove to be relevant despite the many years since they were written. "Do not trouble yourself much to get new things, whether clothes or friends," Thoreau writes in *Walden*. "Turn the old; return to them. Things do not change, we change." The wilderness that Thoreau sought during his life was under attack by deforestation then as now; the commercial impulse in people was strong then as now; the new industrial technologies of the day troubled those who struggled to find their place among them then as now; the government behaved in ways that offended people's consciences then as now. Things have not changed, and so we turn to the old. We return to Thoreau.

CHAPTER ONE

Thoreau's Early Life

Henry Thoreau was born on July 2, 1817, in his grandmother's farmhouse on the outskirts of the small village of Concord, Massachusetts. The Concord of Thoreau's time was a sparsely populated town of two thousand residents. Situated 16 miles (25.7 kilometers) west of Boston, Concord was one of the largest towns in Massachusetts, occupying thirty-six times as much land as Boston, the state's capital. Concord was settled along the Concord River, which flows with the Assabet and Sudbury Rivers and joins the Merrimack River, which in turn flows to the sea. The Concord River provided water for the Middlesex Canal, which connected Boston with the town of Lowell. Its location as the meeting place for several rivers made Concord a natural waypoint for cargo ships carrying lumber and other goods from Maine. However, more than its waterways, Concord

Henry Thoreau was born here, on the second floor of the Wheeler-Minot Farmhouse in Concord, Massachusetts.

was an important crossroads. Roads from Boston met in Concord, and from there, travelers could take one of several roads that spread toward southern Massachusetts, the Berkshires in western Vermont, and New Hampshire to the north.

Everyday Life in Concord

In the nineteenth century, many Concord residents were engaged in agriculture in some way. Farmers grew rye, corn, and potatoes. Some experimented with fruit, especially grapevines, and others

This engraving made during Thoreau's lifetime depicts Concord. Several major roads and rivers converged either in or near Concord, making the small village a bustling hub for regional commerce.

dabbled in cultivating silkworms. Farmers also kept sheep, cows, horses, and oxen. Oxen outnumbered horses over two to one, as they were the preferred draft animals of New England farmers, capable of hauling immense loads and pulling flat-bottomed boats along the canals and rivers.

The emphasis on farming had a dramatic impact on Concord's landscape. In 1830, only one-sixth of the land in Concord was woodland, as a great amount of land had been cleared to serve as either pasture for grazing animals or tillage for crops. The existing stands of trees were small, amounting to only a half-dozen acres (2.4 hectares) or so. In addition to farming, the need for firewood during New England's harsh winters contributed greatly to deforestation. Boston alone required hundreds of thousands of **cords** of firewood annually. In many cases, firewood was being imported from as far away as Maine. Thoreau himself noted that the need for wood in Concord was so great that it was impossible to walk anywhere in the woods without hearing the sound of axes.

Despite the prevalence of farming in Concord, manufacturing was on the rise during Thoreau's lifetime. In the early part of the 1800s, business owners had opened a number of factories in Concord, including a lead pipe factory and a shoe factory. A steam-powered smithy was opened in 1832, and two new banks were opened—one in 1832 and another in 1835. Concord also boasted a number of craftsmen, including clockmakers, milliners (hatmakers), gunsmiths, coopers (people who make barrels), and people who made soap, bricks, and pencils. These manufacturers sold their goods wholesale, meaning that they sold their products in bulk to merchants outside of town, who in turn sold these goods to individual consumers for profit. With travelers from around New England filtering into the village's crossroads and manufacturers shipping products outside of town, Concord was a busy place. Wagons were constantly trundling into and out of town, and travelers and **teamsters** alike stopped to rest in the village's taverns or resupply in its shops.

Concord's history is long, and its residents were proud of their heritage. Established in 1645, Concord was among the first permanent European settlements in Massachusetts. Most of the village's residents were white Protestants, with roots mainly in England or Scotland, who settled long before the start of the American Revolution. From the beginning, Concord was a democratic society: the British government, which granted Concord its charter, left the village largely to its own devices during the colonial period. Political power was shared among a **homogenous** group of white, landowning, male residents who participated in

Reenactors stage the battle of North Bridge in Concord. The first battle of the Revolutionary War was fought in Concord on April 19, 1775.

general assemblies. As the British began encroaching on these liberties in the years leading up to the Revolutionary War, the residents of Concord were among the first to organize militias and take up arms in defense of their rights. The Concord militia fought in the first battle of the Revolution, which took place in Concord and the neighboring town of Lexington on April 19, 1775.

In addition to the white, Anglo-Saxon, and Protestant majority, the town also hosted some recent transplants, including black slaves who had run away from southern plantations and Irish migrants. These groups were typically among the poorest in Concord and lived in shanties far removed from the center of town.

The Thoreaus

Thoreau's family was suited to life in Concord. Like most of the other villagers, the Thoreaus neither enjoyed **exorbitant** wealth nor suffered from abject poverty, though they were at times threatened with bankruptcy. Descended from Scottish and French ancestors, Thoreau was the third of four children born to John Thoreau and Cynthia Dunbar. Named Henry at birth, he was **christened** David six weeks after he was born in honor of his recently deceased uncle, David. For the beginning of his life, Thoreau was called David Henry.

John and Cynthia Thoreau were a study in contrasts. John Thoreau was a short, meek, quiet man, who enjoyed simple pleasures like playing flute in the parish choir and engaging in small talk with friends by the fireside. He was described by his neighbors as "an amiable and most lovable gentleman, but far too honest and scarcely efficiently energetic for this exacting yet not overscrupulous world of ours."

Cynthia Dunbar Thoreau, on the other hand, was a powerful and driven woman. A full foot taller than her husband, Mrs. Thoreau was the dominant personality in the relationship and in the household. Although the Thoreaus often suffered financially, Mrs. Thoreau saw to it that her house was in order and that her children enjoyed good food and a good education. Of her, the neighbors said, "if she had but a crust of bread for dinner, she would see that it was properly served." It rarely came to that. What little the Thoreaus made, they spent it on plenty of food for their family. The remainder they put toward their children's education, enrolling them in the Concord Academy, a local private school.

A compassionate woman by nature, Mrs. Thoreau was active in Concord's social outreach programs. She was a member of the Concord Female Charitable Society, the Bible Society, and the Concord Women's Anti-Slavery Society, which she cofounded. In town, Mrs. Thoreau had a reputation for being outspoken, frank, and gregarious, which led many of her neighbors to see her as an annoying and self-righteous blabbermouth.

As different as John and Cynthia Thoreau were, they both shared a love for nature. Before they had children, the two of them could be spotted hiking around Concord in nearly all seasons. Although the birth of their four children limited their ability to enjoy time alone in nature, they nevertheless sought to impart their passion to their offspring. Mrs. Thoreau frequently called her children to the doorframe of the home to listen to birdsongs, and when they were old enough, she often took them on walks around Concord. These ventures into nature left an impression on young Henry Thoreau. On one such outing, he visited Walden Pond, the location he would one day choose to serve as his headquarters for an experiment in simple living and self-reliance. He wrote:

> [O]ne of the most ancient scenes stamped on the tablets of my memory ... That sweet solitude my spirit seemed so early to require at once gave the preference to this recess among the pines, where almost sunshine and shadow were the only inhabitants that varied the scene, over that tumultuous and varied city, as if it had found its proper nursery.

More often than not, John Thoreau struggled to support his family through his business ventures. Between abandoning a family farm and failing to make a handful of retail stores profitable, John Thoreau was forced to relocate his family several times between Concord and Boston. He finally found limited success when he partnered with an unlikely business companion: his brother-in-law, Charles Dunbar. Dunbar was an undependable and restless bachelor who was unable to hold down a job for any length of time. A frequent houseguest of the Thoreaus, Dunbar would drop in on a lark, stay for weeks or months, then depart just as unexpectedly as he had come in, taking odd jobs up and down New England before returning. Ironically, it was this migratory nature of Dunbar's that led to the Thoreaus' new business venture and their final settlement in Concord.

In 1821, Dunbar stumbled upon a **plumbago** deposit in Bristol, New Hampshire. In the early 1800s, graphite from plumbago mines was being used in the manufacture of a relatively new invention, the pencil. Dunbar's deposit was certified by a Dartmouth College chemistry and mineralogy professor to be of superior quality, beating any that had yet been discovered in the United States. Dunbar staked a claim on the mine and asked his brother-in-law John to set up shop with him in Concord. Thoreau and Dunbar shared the business with a third partner, Cyrus Stow; however, Stow left the business for reasons unknown. Shortly after Stow's departure, Dunbar himself again fell victim to his wanderlust. He, too, quit the business, leaving the pencil company in the hands of John Thoreau.

The Thoreaus' success stemmed from their ability to manufacture a pencil that could write smoothly without the graphite lead crumbling on the page. At the time, the only high-quality pencils were produced by a German company named Faber (today known as Faber-Castell); however, thanks to a new graphite recipe and grinding machine (engineered by Henry David Thoreau himself), the Thoreaus' pencils were the first in the world to rival those coming out of Germany. In 1824, John Thoreau & Co. received a commendation from the Massachusetts Agricultural Society for producing fine-quality pencils. With it came a steady demand for their products.

A sheaf of original Thoreau pencils. The Thoreau family's pencil business found success in their unique graphite formula and manufacturing process, which produced pencils that rivaled those of European pencil producers.

The Road to Higher Learning

Having completed his education at the Concord Academy, Thoreau's family decided to send him to Harvard College (now Harvard University). Located 15 miles (8 km) from Concord in Cambridge, Massachusetts, Harvard was established in 1636 and has offered classes ever since, making it the longest-lived center for higher education in the United States. Initially founded as a divinity school, Harvard initially educated members of the Massachusetts clergy. By the time Thoreau attended classes there, not much had changed. Harvard Divinity School was still the predominant school within the university; however, by then Harvard had also begun to educate future lawyers and medical doctors.

In the early 1830s, the Thoreaus' pencil-making business started to take off. However, between the family business, Cynthia and John's school-teaching salaries, and promised help from Henry's aunts, the family could still only afford to send either Henry or their other son John to college. In 1833, college expenses according to Harvard's catalogue came to just under $190 per academic year. This included tuition, room, board, and textbooks. Tuition was—as it is now at many universities—the most expensive cost associated with attendance, coming to around $55 per year. While textbooks and board were expensive, nearly 10 percent of students' budgets went to firewood to heat their dormitories. In the 1830s, a single open fireplace heated Harvard dormitories with six cords of wood. This came to about twenty-three dollars per year that each student spent on wood. While these expenses may seem like a bargain to modern university students, who often pay upwards of fifty thousand dollars annually for their education, it's important to keep in mind that the average income in 1830s America was much lower, too. Professionals, including doctors and lawyers, could make $1,500 per year only a fraction of what modern-day professionals make), skilled craftsman

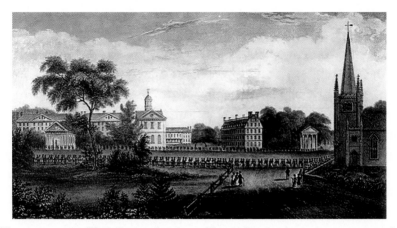

This engraving by Eliza Quincy, daughter of Josiah Quincy, shows the procession of 1836 Harvard alumni across the school's campus.

could make about $400 per year, and first-year schoolteachers only made about $100 per year.

Although many friends of the Thoreau family thought Henry's brother John would be a more promising student, Henry had always demonstrated that he was the more academically inclined of the two. Despite his propensity toward intellectual pursuits, however, Thoreau barely managed to get admitted. He had to take special classes in Greek, Latin, and mathematics in order to get up to speed with Harvard's standards. (While it might seem from these preparatory courses that Thoreau really struggled with his studies, over 90 percent of Harvard students needed to take at least one such course.) Harvard's president, Josiah Quincy, who conducted Thoreau's entrance examinations, told Thoreau that "One branch more, and you had been turned by entirely. You have barely got in."

Even in the 1800s and even for Harvard, a passing grade is a passing grade, no matter how close to failing it may be. Thoreau was admitted. On August 30, 1833, he traveled to Harvard College, where he settled down in the Hollis Hall dormitory, room 20.

Life at Harvard

Today, many students attend universities across the United States with the expectation that they will be free to explore their own course of study while interacting with engaging and talented professors. Unfortunately for Harvard students under Quincy's administration, that ideal was far from reality. In Quincy's own words, the point of higher education was to administer a "thorough drilling." Harvard College, like many other early American centers for higher education, had a fixed curriculum that did not allow for much flexibility during a student's course of study. At Harvard, the study concentrated on the **classics**: three years of Greek, three of Latin, two of mathematics, one of history, three of English, and two of a modern foreign language—German, Italian, Spanish, French, or Portuguese. (By comparison, many modern colleges and universities require students to take only one or two years' worth of obligatory courses.) This curriculum was drawn largely from the college's legacy as a divinity school, preparing students for careers in the clergy more than anything. While the college started to offer elective courses in 1825, they were all but openly discouraged by the administration, which granted only half the academic credit for taking these courses compared to required courses.

Classes themselves were dull affairs. The structure of classes was heavily based on recitations, which discouraged debate and discussion, or even lectures, thought by many modern students to be the epitome of uninspired teaching.

In addition to academic study, dormitories also suffered from plain utilitarianism. Thoreau's dormitory in Hollis Hall featured bare floors, bedsteads made of rough pine, a washstand, two desks, and stiff chairs. The room was heated only by a single fireplace, which had to be carefully stoked to prevent it from going out entirely (matches had not been invented yet). One interesting creature comfort that came with some dormitories was an iron cannonball, which could be heated by the fire to serve as a foot warmer or—for the more mischievous students—kicked down wooden stairs in the dead of night.

In addition to academic regimentation, other areas of college life were all rigidly prescribed. Curfew hours were set, and rules regarding proper dress were strictly enforced. Andrew Peabody, a Harvard student who attended at about the same time as Thoreau and therefore likely shared a similar schedule, noted everyday life at the college:

> Morning prayers were in the summer at six; in winter, about half an hour before sunrise in a bitterly cold chapel. Thence half of each class passed into the several recitation-rooms in the same building ... and three-quarters of an hour later the bell rang for a second set of recitations, including the remaining half of the students. Then came breakfast, which in the college commons consisted solely of coffee, hot rolls, and butter, except when members of a mess had succeeded in pinning to the nether surface of the table, by a two-pronged fork, some slices of meat from the previous day's dinner. Between ten and twelve every student attended another recitation or lecture. Dinner was at half-past twelve—a meal not deficient in quantity, but by no means appetizing to those who had come from neat homes and well-ordered tables. There was another recitation in the afternoon, except on Saturday; then evening prayers at six, or in winter at early twilight; then the evening meal, plain as the breakfast, with tea instead of coffee, and cold bread, of the consistency of wool, for the hot rolls. After tea the dormitories rang with song and merriment till the study-bell, at eight in winter, at nine in summer, sounded the curfew for fun and frolic, proclaiming dead silence throughout the college premises, under penalty of a

domiciliary visit from the officer of the entry, and, in case of a serious offense, of private or public admonition.

Harvard in the early 1800s was clearly a highly structured institution that largely restricted personal expression and fulfillment.

The Reign of Josiah Quincy

Josiah Quincy served as Harvard's president from 1829 to 1845. As a young man, Quincy attended Harvard and studied law. After his college career, Quincy served in the US House of Representatives and as mayor of Boston before being inaugurated as Harvard's fifteenth president.

During his tenure, Quincy introduced the scale of merit, a system for calculating class rank, which determined scholarship awards at the end of the year. Based on educational reforms originally introduced in 1825, Quincy's marking system expanded to govern both academic and social life. Under Quincy's scale, students were eligible to earn a total of eight marks per day based on that day's recitations. These marks were subject to point deductions for an absurd number of violations, including misbehavior, insubordination, absence from morning prayers or classes, and curfew infractions—behavior that practically defines the modern college experience. Professors were often required to supervise their students rather than concentrate on actually educating them. One of Thoreau's contemporaries noted that during morning prayers, a professor sat in a raised "sentry box" over the assembled students and marked the names of the absent and the misbehaving. Quincy's system was so complex and broad that, by some estimates, a typical student could accumulate over fourteen thousand points during the course of their academic career.

To make matters worse, the marking system was cumulative, penalizing students for behavior committed years ago. Furthermore, Quincy calculated these points himself, leading to countless mathematical errors, many of which worked against students.

Between the ridiculousness of the system and the unjustness in its implementation, many students—including Thoreau—developed a disdain for the college and higher education in general. Many students dropped out. The **malaise** as a result of Quincy's influence extended beyond Harvard as well, as many prospective students who had been considering Harvard looked elsewhere.

Thoreau's College Career

When Thoreau arrived at Harvard in the fall of 1833, he had just turned sixteen. Attendance at Harvard at that time hovered around four hundred students. Thoreau's class varied in number during his time there from forty-three to fifty students. Despite struggling with his entrance examinations, Thoreau turned out to be a diligent student. At the beginning of his college career, he was consistently placed at the top of his class. At the end of his first and second years, he was awarded $25 in "exhibition money," or a scholarship, for his high marks. In his second year, he was asked to participate in an honorary conference showcasing the college's best students of that year.

In his junior year, however, Thoreau's academic performance slipped. During his second term that year, a college regulation allowed Thoreau to withdraw from the college and take a teaching position in a country school in order to earn a little money. Because his academic work during this semester was minimal, his class rank fell to the average range. By the third term of that year, Thoreau had fallen ill, suffering from a fit brought on by **tuberculosis**, a bacterial infection that would plague him for the rest of his life. He was forced to leave campus, missing classes in the meantime. His illness lasted through the beginning of his senior year, causing him to slip to twenty-third in his class. In his final term, Thoreau managed to raise his ranking by attending a number of voluntary lectures, graduating in nineteenth place and again securing a $25 scholarship. The ranking system, with its emphasis on attendance over ability

HELL-RAISING IN HARVARD

Thoreau's time at Harvard may have influenced his resistance to authority. Student resistance to the administration of the college was widespread. In March 1834, students from each of the four class years signed a petition to abolish President Quincy's scaling system. Of the thirty-eight names from the first-year class, Thoreau's was among them.

Frustration over Quincy's system boiled over in May 1834, when resistance grew into outward hostility. On May 19, a student in Professor Christopher Dunkin's Greek class stopped in the middle of his recitation and said, "I do not recognize your authority." When asked to apologize to Dunkin, the student instead withdrew. On hearing of the event, the student population exploded with outrage. Overnight, students broke into Professor Dunkin's classroom, breaking furniture and smashing all of the windows. The vandalism amounted to over three hundred dollars (almost double the annual tuition). The following morning, "scraping, whistling, groaning, and other disgraceful noises" interrupted prayers. To prevent further disturbance, a night watchman was ordered to patrol the grounds, but he, too, was harassed by students who pelted him with rocks. Students hung a black flag (the international symbol for piracy) over Holworthy Hall as well as an **effigy** of Quincy from the "Rebellion Tree" that stood in Harvard's courtyard.

The response of Harvard's administration was severe. President Quincy declared that the vandals would be handed over to the Middlesex County Court rather than be subject to college tribunals, as is the custom for universities. The riots were such a problem that the faculty dismissed the entire sophomore class (with only three exceptions). These students would be held back a year and forced to retake their entrance examinations and produce letters of good conduct. Several members from other class years, including from Thoreau's freshman class, were also dismissed from campus.

Although Thoreau doesn't seem to have participated in what became known as the Dunkin Rebellion, he did come to the defense of one of his schoolmates, Giles Henry Whitney, who was singled out for disrupting morning prayers and dismissed for five months. Thoreau both testified in Whitney's hearing and wrote a letter on his behalf to the administration. Although Thoreau was not prepared to participate in open rebellion, he did take civil action to correct what he saw as a miscarriage of justice.

Harvard's fifteenth president, Josiah Quincy, instituted the scale of merit, a draconian system of ranking students according to strict adherence to academic and social rules. Quincy's system was so despised by the students that it once led to open rebellion on campus.

and its cumulative nature, worked against Thoreau; had he not been subject to Quincy's scale of merit, he would have likely finished with a higher class rank than he did.

Given the nature of Harvard at the time and the way Thoreau fell victim to the arbitrary marking system, it's no wonder that college life left a bad taste in his mouth. Years after he graduated, Thoreau complained of Harvard. When Thoreau's friend Ralph Waldo Emerson later tried to encourage Thoreau that his time at Harvard had taught him all the branches of learning, Thoreau said, "[Y]es, indeed, all the branches and none of the roots." According to Thoreau, higher education (at least insofar as it was structured in his time) was merely a shallow exploration into knowledge that depended on conformity and rote learning.

Not all was bad at Harvard for Thoreau, however. As dispiriting as the classroom experience could be, Thoreau reveled in the opportunity to explore the stacks of the college's library. In the 1830s, Harvard's library totaled fifty thousand volumes, and students were permitted to withdraw as many of them as they wished. Thoreau, who had a near compulsion to read every book available to him, made good use of this exceptional resource, diving deeply into the work of writers such as John Milton, Samuel Johnson, William Shakespeare, Geoffrey Chaucer, Homer, the ancient Greek and Anglo-Saxon poets, and many more. Also among the books Thoreau withdrew from Harvard's library was a small book simply titled *Nature*, written by a recent Concord transplant named Ralph Waldo Emerson. This book and its author would later become major influences on his life. As much as Thoreau valued the access he had in Harvard's library, however, he later wrote in *Walden* that the seclusion he found in the woods was superior to reading in a university library: "My residence was more favorable, not only to thought, but to serious reading, than a university."

Wisely acknowledging that this nearly unlimited access was temporary, Thoreau kept a series of notebooks called **commonplace books**, in which he recorded quotations from his readings so that he could have them close at hand for the rest of his life. Thoreau's surviving commonplace books amount to six thousand printed pages. Many of the quotes Thoreau had

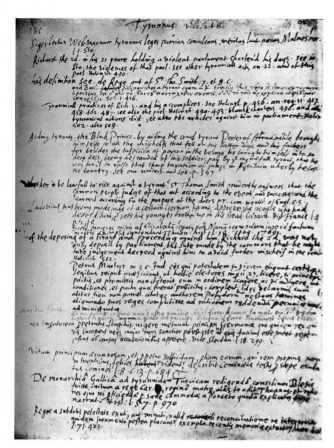

During his time at Harvard, Thoreau got into the habit of keeping a commonplace book. Much like this one from English poet John Milton, Thoreau's commonplace book catalogued quotes and other notes from his reading for future use.

copied during his college years later worked their way into his essays well after graduation.

In addition to the vast library available to him, Thoreau also admitted that another benefit to attending Harvard was the opportunity to study English under Edward Tyrrel Channing. Professor Channing required his students to write thematic papers, which are essays that address a particular topic. Thoreau's papers showed a flair and aptitude that later led Channing to permit Thoreau to write on topics of his own choosing. Over the course of three years studying under Channing, Thoreau admitted, he found a writing style with which he could express himself.

CHAPTER TWO

Revealing the Writer

T horeau completed his classes at Harvard in the spring of 1837, and the graduation ceremony was scheduled for August 30. At that time, college commencement ceremonies were held at the start of the following fall term rather than the end of the graduating class's final term in spring. In the preceding weeks, Thoreau enjoyed a summer vacation staying with his friend Charles Stearns Wheeler in a hut on the banks of Flint's Pond that Wheeler had built himself. The two spent these weeks between classes and graduation reading, relaxing, and sleeping, which went a long way toward recuperating Thoreau's health following his battle with tuberculosis. In later years, Thoreau recalled his summer in the hut happily, and his experience certainly inspired his later experiment at Walden Pond.

Crayon portrait of Henry David Thoreau, drawn by Samuel Worcester Rowse in 1854. Thoreau is shown in his mid-thirties.

At graduation, Thoreau was invited by virtue of his class rank to contribute to an honorary conference on commercialism in modern America. Thoreau's speech on the subject would prove **prototypical** of his later philosophy on wealth, nature, and life:

> We are to look chiefly for the origin of the commercial spirit, and the power that still cherishes and sustains it, in a blind and unmanly love of wealth. Wherever this exists, it is too sure to become the ruling spirit; and, as a natural consequence, it infuses into all our thoughts and affections a degree of its own selfishness; we become selfish in our patriotism, selfish in domestic relations, selfish in our religion.
>
> Let men, true to their natures, cultivate the moral affections, lead manly and independent lives; let them make riches the means and not the ends of existence, and we shall hear no more of the commercial spirit ... This curious world which we inhabit is more wonderful than convenient; more beautiful than it is useful; it is more to be admired and enjoyed than used. The order of things should be somewhat reversed; the seventh should be man's day of toil, wherein to earn his living by the sweat of his brow; and the other six a Sabbath of the affections and the soul—in which to range this widespread garden, and drink in the soft influences and sublime revelations of nature.

There is a common legend that Thoreau refused to accept his diploma during his commencement. The roots of this story are in a letter Thoreau had written to Ralph Waldo Emerson in 1847, in which he said, "They have been foolish enough to put at the end of all this earnest the old joke of a diploma. Let every sheep keep but his own skin, I say." (Thoreau was punning off the fact that, at that time, diplomas were printed on sheepskin.) While Thoreau did refuse a diploma from Harvard, it was not his bachelor's degree diploma, of which there are copies. Rather, Thoreau disregarded an offer of a master's degree from Harvard. In the 1800s, master's degrees were handed out to alumni of the college who survived three years after graduation and were willing to give a donation of $5. It was purely a moneymaking scheme on the part of the college, and Thoreau would not participate in it.

Master Thoreau

In the 1800s, a college graduate like Thoreau had his pick of one of four careers: the clergy, law, medicine, or school teaching. With no interest in the other three, Thoreau chose teaching. Many members of his family, including his father, maternal grandfather, brother John, and sister Helen, had taught school. Fortunately for Thoreau, he already had an offer to teach at the Concord Center School when he graduated from Harvard. They offered him a salary of $500 per year. Many of his classmates did not have the benefit of any position waiting for them at all, let alone one as well paying as Thoreau's.

The Concord Center School was situated in a small brick building in the village square. Its enrollment totaled ninety students, and had they all attended at the same time, they would hardly have fit in the squat schoolhouse. Fortunately for Thoreau, only fifty-two of those enrolled attended during his winter as teacher, but even then the place was cramped.

Thoreau was not long for the Concord Center School. In addition to the stress of educating more than fifty rowdy farm boys with no interest in learning, he also had pressure from the school committee to discipline his students. At that time, the use of **corporal punishment** on students was not only permitted but required. At the end of his second week teaching, one of the members of the school committee criticized Thoreau because his classroom was not as quiet as hoped and he did not beat his students. The committee member

Caning was a popular form of corporal punishment in nineteenth-century classrooms. Many educators believed there was no better way to ensure discipline among their students. Thoreau begged to differ.

took Thoreau into the hallway and insisted that it was his duty to use physical punishment to maintain control of his classroom.

Thoreau, always ahead of his time, resented the command, which he considered barbaric and inhumane. To underscore the absurdity of the committee member's insistence, he went into his classroom, chose six students at random, and whipped each of them with a ruler. The students were understandably confused and harbored ill will toward their schoolmaster. Said student Daniel Potter years later, "When I went to my seat, I was so mad that I said to myself: 'When I'm grown up, I'll whip you for this, old feller.' But I never saw the day I wanted to do it.—Why, Henry Thoreau was the kindest hearted of men." Because of this kindheartedness, Thoreau refused to work in the school that insisted on such treatment of its students. That night, he tendered his resignation to the school committee. Thoreau was unemployed after less than two weeks.

The Panic of 1837

Complicating Thoreau's decision to resign his position was a period of economic recession known as the Panic of 1837. In the aftermath of America's war with Great Britain in 1812, the United States experienced a period of booming economic growth. During this time, Americans enjoyed the benefits of widely available **credit**. The US Treasury tripled the amount of paper money in circulation, going from $51 million to $149 million. In 1836, however, that rapid growth ended when the wheat crop failed. The cost of bread went up, and the price of cotton fell by half. Complicating matters, America's **creditors**, who were mostly British at the time, started refusing loan payments made with US dollars, demanding payments in gold instead.

American businesses crumbled almost overnight. Over a two-week span, several large New York-based merchants collapsed, amounting to over $100 million worth of failures. (To put that in perspective, the entire budget for the US federal government during

WHAT'S IN A NAME?
INDIVIDUALITY.

Quitting his job as a schoolteacher after less than two weeks was not the only self-directed change that Thoreau made in the months following his graduation. In 1837, Thoreau took to referring to himself and signing his name as Henry David Thoreau, reversing the order of his christened name.

Just as when he chose to leave his position as a schoolteacher, those who knew Thoreau had strong opinions about his decision to change his name. For one, he did not go through the official channels to have his name changed. At that time, those wishing to change their names were required to submit a formal petition to the Massachusetts legislature. Thoreau did none of that. He simply changed his name by himself, signing his name as Henry David Thoreau. This frustrated the people of Concord, who thought that his christened name of David Henry, the name by which they had come to know him, should have been enough for him. Even after Thoreau's death, a Concord farmer is reported to have said, "Henry D. Thoreau—Henry D. Thoreau … His name ain't no more Henry D. Thoreau than my name is Henry D. Thoreau. And everybody knows it, and he knows it. His name's Da-a-vid Henry and it ain't never been nothing but Da-a-vid Henry. And he knows that!" For years afterward, his neighbors continued to call him David Henry out of protest, but Thoreau was just as determined. Whenever someone called him David Henry, he corrected them.

The exact reasons for Thoreau's choice is relatively unclear. Perhaps he thought that Henry David simply had a better ring to it. Another reason may owe to his characteristic contrarian individuality, informed in large part by his experience reading Ralph Waldo Emerson. In *Nature*, which Thoreau read twice in college, Emerson wrote, "Our age is retrospective. It builds the sepulchers of the fathers. It writes biographies, histories, and criticism. The foregoing generations beheld God and nature face to face; we, through their eyes. Why should not we also enjoy an original relation to the universe?" Perhaps Thoreau was applying Emerson's theory of individual experience by altering his association with the deceased and reversing the order of his name to Henry David Thoreau. He would no longer be called first by a dead man's name.

this time was only $37 million.) Those that survived the initial **culling** were forced to raise their prices in order to stave off a slow financial death. Furthermore, with the availability of easy credit during the boom years, many private individuals had gone deep into debt to finance their livelihoods; now, their creditors were looking to collect, and the paper money that was in abundance was considered to be nearly worthless.

Without a job and without any real prospects, Thoreau's friends and family wondered how he could abandon a respectable position with a decent salary. However, Thoreau had made his choice between respecting his conscience and obeying popular notions of practicality; to him, conscience must always win out.

Ralph Waldo Emerson

Throughout the fall and winter of 1837–1838, Thoreau looked for a teaching job to no avail. At first focusing his search in Massachusetts, it became clear to him that he would have to widen his scope. Over the months, Thoreau sent out numerous letters to schools and contacts, including President Quincy at Harvard, expressing his interest in securing another teaching position. Quincy alerted Thoreau to an opening in Kentucky, but when Thoreau applied, he was rejected. He also traveled north through Maine but found nothing there, either.

The final months of 1837 were not a total waste, however; indeed, during this time Thoreau made a connection that would amount to not only the most important friendship of his life but one of the greatest friendships in history. In the winter of 1837, he met Ralph Waldo Emerson.

Ralph Waldo Emerson was born on May 25, 1803, in Boston. Descended from a long line of clergymen, Emerson studied divinity at Harvard and was later ordained in the **Unitarian** Church in 1829. Emerson's experience in the church was short-lived, however; his wife, Ellen Tucker, died of tuberculosis in 1831—just two years after they were married. Grief-stricken, Emerson started to question some

Ralph Waldo Emerson proved to be an invaluable lifetime friend of Thoreau's.

of the religion's teachings and sacraments. He ultimately resigned his pastorate in 1832.

In the wake of his wife's death, Emerson voyaged to Europe, where he spent time with several of the great **Romantic** poets: Samuel Taylor Coleridge and William Wordsworth of England, and Thomas Carlyle of Scotland. When Emerson returned to the United States a year later, his attention turned from the religious to science and natural history. He moved to Concord, where much of his family was from. In 1835, Emerson remarried and settled into "Coolidge Castle" on Lexington Road with his wife, Lydia Jackson.

In Concord, Emerson started a new career in public lecturing, facilitated by the spread of the **lyceum movement** in the mid-1820s. The goal of the movement was community education, and it drew its name from the Lyceum, a garden in ancient Athens where Aristotle held his classes on philosophy. Each lyceum was designed to be a center for its community's intellectual life. In addition to featuring lectures and debates on a range of topics, including science, morality, and history, lyceums also hosted dramatic productions and classes. At first, each community's lyceum featured its own local scholars and lecturers. However, as the movement grew and more lyceums started cropping up throughout the United States, they began partnering with one another to exchange speakers. This ultimately grew into complex lecture circuits. Many of these lyceums continued to function into the early twentieth century.

The first lyceum in the United States was the Millbury Branch Number 1 of the American Lyceum, which was founded in 1826 in Millbury, Massachusetts, by Josiah Holbrook. Soon, other lyceums started to spring up around Massachusetts and the United States. On January 17, 1829, the doors of the Concord Lyceum—one of the largest and longest-lived of its kind—opened. Emerson's fame as a lecturer grew quickly, owing to such popular and influential essays and speeches as "Self-Reliance" and "The American Scholar," which was delivered to Thoreau's graduating class at Harvard. Before long,

TRANSCENDENTALISM

In addition to fueling Thoreau's interest in pursuing writing as a profession, Emerson also introduced him to the budding American philosophy known as **Transcendentalism**, of which Emerson was in many ways the leader.

Transcendentalism grew out of a reaction against the ideas and theories that had become popular as a result of the **Enlightenment**, in particular the theory of knowledge proposed by the English philosopher John Locke. According to Locke, the human mind at birth is a *tabula rasa*, Latin for "blank slate," onto which knowledge is etched as the person ages and learns. Knowledge can only be gleaned through the five senses—seeing, hearing, tasting, touching, and smelling. Locke's theory was hugely influential, with people from theologians to political philosophers incorporating his ideas into their own philosophies. His theory also directly led to the development of the scientific method, which is still in use today as a means of determining fact in all of the hard sciences, such as biology, chemistry, and physics.

Despite the prevalence of Locke's theories, many philosophers, especially the eighteenth-century German idealist philosophers Immanuel Kant and Georg Wilhelm Friedrich Hegel, began to question the limits of Locke's work. To them, some knowledge is innately understood by the human mind and, thus, *transcends* the senses (hence, the coining of the American movement inspired by this philosophy as Transcendentalism). This knowledge was the voice of God in man, which manifested in man's moral sense, his conscience, and in the experience of the "over-soul," a universal understanding that individuals can tap into. This theory placed a greater emphasis on intuition, imagination, and individuality over empirical experience.

In the 1830s, this philosophical thought, called German idealism, arrived in New England through its adoption by intellectuals such as Emerson, Reverend Orestes Bronson, Margaret Fuller, and Thoreau. Initially brought together by a conference on idealist philosophy hosted by Harvard College, many of these New England intellectuals decided to periodically meet informally to discuss their own ideas and reactions. Calling themselves the Hedge Club, they frequently chose Emerson's house in Concord as their headquarters. Newspapers of the day called them the Transcendentalists.

The Transcendentalists believed there was more to the world than what could be seen, heard, smelled, touched, and tasted. To them, the natural world also contained spiritual truths that transcended the senses.

Thoreau joined the club in the fall of 1837. Although he rarely shaped the philosophy as many others did, he nevertheless benefitted greatly from the discussion and readily accepted most of the philosophy's major tenets. Much of his greatest work, including his experiment in Walden Pond, was greatly influenced by Transcendentalist ideals, and he remained its most stalwart believer until the end of his life.

he was among the most influential thinkers in all of New England. However, his prominence came at a price: living in the small town of Concord, Emerson often wanted for a companion who had a similarly sharp mind.

Thoreau had been exposed to Emerson as early as 1835, when Emerson, a member of the committee of the Harvard Board of Overseers, was invited to the college to examine Thoreau's sophomore class on rhetoric. Although Emerson had a habit of seeking out intelligent, talented young people like Thoreau, neither recorded in their journals any sort of impression that the one had left on the other. However, Thoreau did seem to be taken with Emerson's ideas. In the spring term of 1837, he twice withdrew Emerson's book *Nature* from the Harvard library. Although Thoreau's commonplace books do not suggest he read much of Emerson later in his life, *Nature* unquestionably became one of the most formative books he had ever read. Later that year, Emerson wrote to President Quincy encouraging him to award Thoreau a scholarship.

When Thoreau returned to Concord after graduation, he and Emerson knew each other only as acquaintances. Shortly after, though, they struck up a great friendship. Accounts on how exactly they came to be personally connected vary, leaving the question up for speculation. According to Emerson, his sister-in-law, Mrs. Brown, once boarded with the Thoreaus. While there, she discovered some of Henry's poems, which she told Emerson about. Another account states that one of Henry's sisters directed Mrs. Brown to a note in Henry's journals that seemed to anticipate something Emerson would say in one of his lectures. In any event, Emerson became familiar with Thoreau through his early work and thinking, and from there their friendship began.

Emerson and Thoreau

Thoreau found in Emerson what he believed to be lacking in his own father, John. Whereas John Thoreau was passive and simple, Emerson was bold and fiercely intelligent. Thoreau would later write

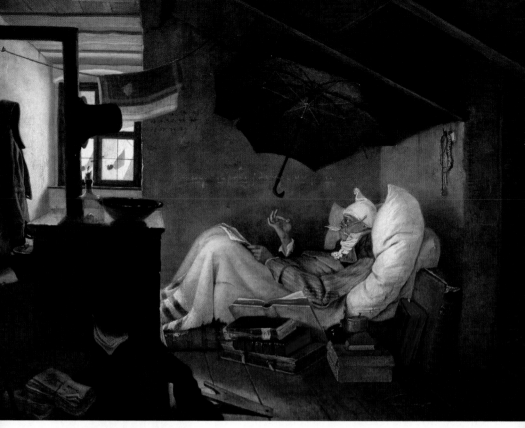

The Poor Poet, painted by Carl Spitzweg. Thoreau wrote at the beginning of his journal that he sought a garret, or attic, like this one that he could rent cheaply and devote himself to his craft.

that he "found in Emerson a world where turns existed with the same perfection as the objects he studied in external nature, his ideals real and exact as antennae and stamina." Emerson offered Thoreau leadership and companionship through a life of the mind, especially by opening up his personal library to him. As at Harvard, Thoreau was again thrilled to have an expansive and deep collection of volumes to pursue through. Many of the books he found there, especially Emerson's large collection of Asian writings and Buddhist scriptures, informed Thoreau's later work.

Furthermore, Emerson kick-started Thoreau's interest in pursuing writing as a profession, by encouraging him in the fall of 1837 to keep a journal. On October 22, Thoreau started his journal, writing, "'What are you doing now?' he asked. 'Do you keep a journal?' So I make my first entry to-day."

Thoreau and Emerson's relationship seemed to many outside observers to be hierarchical, with Emerson taking a dominating mentor position over Thoreau. Emerson was fourteen years Thoreau's senior and the more successful of the two, having made a name for himself across New England through his lectures. This led many, including later biographers, to believe that Thoreau sat in the shade of Emerson's shadow, and that many of his writings were heavily influenced by Emerson if not borrowed outright from his work. In Concord, Thoreau suffered under this perception his whole life, and it contributed largely to the delay in appreciating his literary achievements on the part of later readers, critics, and scholars.

Despite this common evaluation of the nature of their relationship, Emerson and Thoreau considered themselves to be equals in their friendship. The one was always just as interested in the other. In 1838, Emerson wrote to his cousin that when the famous Scottish writer Thomas Carlyle came to Massachusetts, "I expect to introduce Thoreau to him as *the* man of Concord."

Passion and Profession

After an unsuccessful year of searching for a position as a schoolteacher, Thoreau

Unable to find employment teaching elsewhere, Thoreau took over the Concord Academy in 1838. Along with his brother John, Thoreau shaped his school into a place of serious study without the need for corporal punishment.

finally determined to create his own. In June 1838, Thoreau opened a private school out of his family's home and arranged with his parents to let his pupils board with them. After the first month, Thoreau only had four students. Later that year, however, the master of Concord Academy retired, and Thoreau made an arrangement to rent the building for five dollars each quarter and take over operation of the academy. As before, attracting students was a slow process. In October, Thoreau looked to abandon this new venture, but again found that no other school but his own would employ him, so he remained at Concord Academy.

That winter, enough students had enrolled at Concord Academy that Thoreau asked his brother John to join him as a second instructor. John Thoreau added to the school's viability due to the increased amount of subjects the brothers could teach together. John would teach English and mathematics, and Henry would teach the classics as well as French, physics, natural philosophy, and natural history. The Thoreau brothers eventually enrolled twenty-five students at Concord Academy, the maximum they wished to instruct. At one point, there was a waiting list of students who hoped to get in.

By all accounts, the Thoreau brothers were kind yet disciplined schoolmasters. They charged their students four dollars per quarter for English instruction with an additional two dollars per quarter for classical languages. If a family struggled to make tuition payments, the Thoreaus offered them a full-tuition scholarship. They also managed to avoid doling out corporal punishment by asking their pupils why they wanted to study before making them pledge to honor the academy's rules. If any of the students misbehaved or neglected their studies, the Thoreaus reminded them of their agreement.

Although Thoreau had finally found a steady and successful teaching position—one of his own making—he was nevertheless dissatisfied with his profession. While it served to keep him clothed and fed, he never imagined it to be his life's work. "What may a man do and not be ashamed of it?" he wrote. "He may not do nothing, surely." His passion instead lay in writing, which Ralph Waldo Emerson eagerly encouraged.

The bulk of Thoreau's writing during this time period was captured in his journals. Over his lifetime, Thoreau wrote over two million words in his journals; set in print, his volumes amount to seven thousand pages. From the beginning, Thoreau's journals focused on his pursuit of writing as an art. They featured notes on form, editing, and revision, as well as quotations from his readings, random ponderings, observations in nature, poems, and comments that he would cut out and recopy into his later essays and books.

At this time, Thoreau endeavored to make himself a poet. To Thoreau, the purpose of poetry was to express the emotions experienced by the poet—as he said, "[T]he poem is drawn out from under the feet of the poet—his whole weight has rested on this ground." Together with his desire to express pure emotion, Thoreau incorporated Transcendental philosophy with natural philosophy to create such lines as this quatrain:

> I am bound, I am bound, for a distant shore,
> By a lonely isle, by a far Azore,
> There it is, there it is, the treasure I seek,
> On the barren sands of a desolate creek.

His early attempts at poetry were enthusiastically celebrated by Emerson, who called his work "the purest strain, the loftiest, I think, that has yet pealed from this unpoetic American forest."

The *Dial*

Many of the members of the Hedge Club, like Emerson and Thoreau, were also writers; however, they discovered that their work was frequently stonewalled from publication in the most popular literary magazines. To the editors of the day, the Transcendentalists wrote drivel that ran counter to the work produced by the more popular poets of the time. Frustrated, the Transcendentalists agreed

Margaret Fuller was a member of the Hedge Club and served as the first editor for the club's short-lived literary magazine, the *Dial*.

in May 1840 that they would publish their own magazine. Like Thoreau had done with Concord Academy, the Transcendentalists were determined to exercise their individuality and shape the world according to their own desires. Hedge Club associate Margaret Fuller agreed to serve as editor. On July 1, 1840, the first issue of the Hedge Club's periodical, named the *Dial*, was published.

The *Dial*, however, would not prove to be as successful as the Thoreau brothers' academy. Nearly two years into the publication, Fuller resigned as editor. The magazine struggled to reach a wider audience. At its peak, its circulation totaled one thousand copies, and only three hundred people subscribed to it. As a result, it did not bring in any money for its contributors or its editor, who was forced to work for hours on end day after day to bring each issue to print. When no one else came forward to assume the responsibility, Emerson reluctantly took over.

Under Fuller's editorship, Thoreau struggled to find a home for his work. Over the two years of its operation, he had only placed four short poems and a translation within its pages even though Emerson constantly badgered Fuller to feature his friend. Now in charge, Emerson endeavored to realize his vision of spreading Thoreau's work to a wider audience. In the October 1842 edition of the *Dial*, Emerson featured eight of Thoreau's poems. Within a few short months, the number of Thoreau's published works had doubled.

Emerson's enthusiasm for his friend's work quickly waned, however. As the fall of 1842 wore on, Thoreau's work became increasingly insular. He disregarded established poetic conventions, such as regular meter and rhyme, in the interest of satisfying his own creative impulses. As much as the Transcendentalists valued individuality, few of them were impressed with Thoreau's work during this time. Even Emerson started to discourage Thoreau's poetry, suggesting that he submit translations instead. "Their fault is," Emerson wrote in his journal, "that the gold does not yet flow pure, but is drossy and crude. The thyme and marjoram are not yet made into honey; the assimilation is imperfect." Elsewhere, Emerson wrote that one of Thoreau's poems, "A Winter Walk," "makes me nervous and wretched to read it, with all its merits." At one point, Thoreau was so disheartened by his friend's criticism that he burned many of his poetry manuscripts, an act he later regretted.

The *Dial* eventually folded after it printed its last issue in April 1844. The problems of circulation and income that Fuller had experienced persisted through Emerson's tenure, and it was becoming difficult to simply make enough to meet its own costs of printing. Those who read it more often than not disparaged it, and even the Transcendentalists frequently expressed their disappointment in the project. For Thoreau, however, his experience writing for the *Dial* proved invaluable to his self-confidence. During the magazine's four years in print, he published thirty-one poems, essays, and translations. Placing one's work in any publication is a boon to young writers. Now that the *Dial* had finished, he turned his attention to writing for an even wider audience.

CHAPTER THREE

⌣

Walden

Thoreau's most famous volume of writing is entitled *Walden: or, Life in the Woods*. It documents his experience living alone for two years and two months in a one-room cabin that he constructed along the banks of Walden Pond in Concord. Arriving on July 4, 1845, his move to Walden Pond was a declaration of independence achieved by a retreat into solitude. In the book's second chapter, Thoreau poetically states his reasons for going off to live by himself:

> I went to the woods because I wished to live deliberately, to front only the essential facts of life, and see if I could not learn what it had to teach, and not, when I came to die, discover that I had not lived. I did not wish to live what was not life, living is so dear; nor did I wish to practice resignation, unless it

Following the death of his brother John, Thoreau wished to find the solitude and peace needed to finish his book recounting their trip on the Concord and Merrimack Rivers. Thoreau found just that and more along the banks of Walden Pond.

was quite necessary. I wanted to live deep and suck out the marrow of life, to live so sturdily and Spartan-like as to put to rout all that was not life, to cut a broad swath and shave close, to drive life into a corner, and reduce it to its lowest terms.

His experiment, as he liked to call it, had as its goal both understanding the fundamentals of life as well as learning how to live well. At Walden, Thoreau hoped to live as simply as possible and with the least possible exertion. With those so-called "necessaries of life" managed, he would be free to read deeply, write, and explore the fundamental questions of life.

The Road to Walden Pond

As early as the fall of 1841, Thoreau had designs to avoid society by living in a cabin in the woods. On Christmas Eve of that year, he wrote in his journal, "I want to go soon and live away by the pond, where I shall hear only the wind whispering among the reeds. It will be a success if I shall have left myself behind. But my friends ask what I will do when I get there. Will it not be employment enough to watch the progress of the seasons?" The pond he was thinking of was not Walden but rather Flint's Pond, where four years earlier he and his friend had spent their summer vacation after college reading and relaxing in a hut. The following day, Christmas, he wrote, "I don't want to feel as if my life were a sojourn any longer. It is time now that I begin to live."

Ironically, Thoreau's wish to find quiet and solitude started to materialize not while at home in Concord but in the bustling heart of New York City. In the spring of 1843, Thoreau had been suffering in nearly every way: physically, emotionally, and intellectually. In January 1842, Thoreau's brother John died suddenly of **tetanus** when he cut a piece of his finger off with a shaving razor, and the wound became seriously infected. Thoreau fell into a deep

Thoreau discovered he was ill suited to the crowded, chaotic energy that coursed through nineteenth-century New York City.

depression as a result. Complicating matters was Thoreau's own poor health, as he was again beset with complications arising from his chronic tuberculosis. Looking for change, Thoreau left Concord for New York to take a position as a tutor for the son of Ralph Waldo Emerson's brother, William Emerson. William Emerson agreed to furnish a room for his son's tutor in their home on Staten Island. In addition to earning some more money and finally living somewhere other than his parents' home or away at college, Thoreau also hoped that living near New York City would help him break into the publishing scene.

For practically all of the United States' history, as today, New York has been the country's busiest and most populous city. New York was the second-most populous city in the United States after Philadelphia at the end of the Revolutionary War; however, by the time the federal government had organized the first census, New York **supplanted** Philadelphia as the nation's largest city with 33,131 residents. Over the next few decades, New York's population swelled. By 1840, New York's population was 312,710, well over three times the population of the country's second-largest city, Baltimore. When Thoreau arrived in the city, it had already taken on the manmade appearance that defines it today, with towering brick buildings and paved streets. Comparing the sidewalks of New York to the earthen paths of his native Concord, Thoreau wrote in a letter to his parents that the city's streets were "clear brick and stone and [provided] no give to the foot."

Then as now, the city's population pulsed and surged at all hours. Some people consider this energy to be a positive feature of New York, but others, including Thoreau, are put ill at ease by the mass and chaos of it all. Thoreau came to dislike the industry and people of New York, who seemed constantly involved in the meanest form of living without considering life's higher purposes. He wrote:

> I don't like the city better, the more I see it, but worse. I am ashamed of my eyes that behold it. It is a thousand times meaner than I could have imagined. It will be something to hate—that's the advantage it will be to me; and even the best people in it are a part of it and talk coolly about it. The pigs in the street are the most respectable part of the population. When will the world learn that a million men are of no importance compared with *one* man?

Staten Island, where Thoreau made his lodging, was not much better in his mind. Although Staten Island was mostly farmland at that time and therefore offered a break from the comings and goings of the city, he nevertheless missed his hometown: "I have hardly begun to lie on Staten Island yet; but like the man who, when forbidden to tread on English ground, carried Scottish ground in his boots, I carry Concord dust in my boots and in my hat—and am I not made of Concord dust?"

Furthermore, the change in climate did little for his health. For weeks after his arrival, he suffered from both a cold and bronchitis. On top of that, Thoreau did not get along with his hosts. He found his pupil to be uninspiring, and he and William Emerson, who was a judge, did not get along. Emerson was a conventional man who had little patience for Thoreau's individualism. Still worse, Thoreau had little success publishing in New York.

Although Thoreau was not one for holidays, he decided to make the trip home for Thanksgiving in 1843. Ralph Waldo Emerson offered Thoreau a place to lecture at the Concord Lyceum if he returned, and Thoreau accepted. During his time back home, Thoreau realized where he was meant to spend his life. The next time he left for Staten Island, on December 3, it was only to gather his belongings at William Emerson's home and conclude his business with the family. Thoreau stayed in Concord for the rest of his life, leaving only for brief trips.

Walden

In the years immediately following his New York City experiment, Thoreau moved back in with his parents. Far from a freeloader, Thoreau, now twenty-six, made regular payments to his parents for his boarding. Thoreau also went to work at the family's pencil business, where he made many profitable improvements to the company's production process. Thanks in large part to their son's contributions, the Thoreaus felt that their business was now profitable enough to warrant building a home of their own rather than renting, as they had always done. They chose a spot on Texas Street and purchased three-quarters of an acre (0.3 ha) from the landowner. Thoreau pitched in to help with the construction, acquiring valuable experience in house building—skills that would soon prove very useful to him.

Although Thoreau found greater peace back home in Concord than he had in New York, he was still frustrated in his literary pursuits. For years, he had wanted to write a book chronicling a boating trip he and his deceased brother John had taken on the Concord and Merrimack Rivers, but he struggled to get the words down. By the fall of 1844, Thoreau had already gone through his material for the third time. He sought to implement the scheme he had proposed at his college commencement, wherein each week he would work one day for his sustenance and write the other six days. However, unless he managed to "get away from it all," the book would never be written.

Thoreau got his chance to do exactly that in the spring of 1845. On March 5, Thoreau's friend William Ellery Channing, a fellow Transcendentalist then living in New York City, wrote to him, "I see nothing for you in this earth but that field which I once christened 'Briars'; go out upon that, build yourself a hut, and there begin the grand process of devouring yourself alive." He was referring to the woods near Walden Pond, a small glacial lake two miles (3 km) south of Concord Village.

Ralph Waldo Emerson had purchased much of the land near Walden Pond six months earlier, in September 1844. Emerson's purchase included an 11-acre (4.5 ha) field for $8.10 per acre as well as approximately 4 acres (1.6 ha) of woodland adjacent to the pond, which included part of the shoreline, for an additional $125. Both Emerson and Thoreau had spent a great deal of time in the forests near Walden Pond, and Emerson most likely purchased the lot to preserve it from woodcutters. Emerson himself had designs on building a writing cabin there. At one point, Emerson wrote to Thomas Carlyle, "One of these days, if I should have any money, I may build me a cabin or a turret there high as the treetops and spend my nights as well as days in the midst of a beauty which never fades for me." However, before Emerson could make good on his wish, Thoreau approached him with designs to stay on Emerson's land. Inspired by Ellery Channing's letter, Thoreau wished to build his own residence on Emerson's land. Emerson gave his friend permission. In late March 1845, Thoreau borrowed an axe and went to work clearing a space among the pines for his home.

Home

Thoreau chose to build his cabin a few feet from a cove on Walden Pond and along one of the main roads into the village. Although there is a perception that Thoreau's experiment at Walden Pond was an escape from society into pure wilderness, this wasn't exactly the case. Thoreau was only after a simulated wilderness, one that could afford him enough solitude to get his work done as was needed. Concord was only about 2 miles (3.2 km) away, and the new house his family had built was closer than that. During the construction of his cabin and planting field at Walden, he stayed with his family, walking each day to the site. Once he was comfortably set up in his new abode, he continued to frequently walk back to his family home for Sunday dinners, where it was said he would raid the family's cookie jar. Often, his mother or sisters brought pies and other sweets to his cabin themselves. Rather than living without society, as many people mistakenly believed, Thoreau merely sought to live just outside of it.

Thoreau's work at Walden Pond involved cutting down pine trees where he wished to place his cabin. He hewed these trees with his borrowed axe into 6-foot (1.8 meter) square timbers, which he used as the studs and rafters. By mid-April, the frame was ready. That month, he purchased a shanty from an Irish laborer named James Collins, who had worked on the Fitchburg Railroad, located near the site of the cabin. Thoreau took down Collins' house to use its boards for his siding and salvaged many of the nails. In May, he invited some of his neighbors to help set up the frame and raise the roof. Afterward, Thoreau went to work clearing a field and planting 2.5 acres (1 hectare) of beans, potatoes, corn, peas, and turnips, of which a

A scale replica of Thoreau's cabin is located a stone's throw away from Thoreau's original site at Walden Pond.

fraction he would eat and the remainder he would sell. On Independence Day, 1845, Thoreau moved in. At that time, the house was still unfinished. It lacked a chimney, a fireplace, and plaster on the interior walls, and the outer walls still had large chinks in them. While it would work fine during the warm summer months, Thoreau would have to work the rest of the season to prepare his home for winter.

When it was completed, Thoreau's house measured 10 feet by 15 feet (3 m by 4.6 m), with windows on the two longer sides. Along one of the shorter sides sat a fireplace made of salvaged brick that was mortared with sand from the pond, and opposite that was the door. The cabin also featured a loft and a small closet. Thoreau placed what few belongings he had in his small home. His furniture, most of which he had made himself, included a bed, a table, a desk, three chairs, a 3-inch (7.6-centimeter) mirror, and a lamp. When he wanted to clean his cabin, he simply put all of his furniture out of doors, washed the floors with pond water and sand as an abrasive, waited for the **slurry** to dry, and swept the floors clean. The whole process

Thoreau built his cabin at Walden Pond himself, making sure that it fit all of his needs as simply as possible. Measuring just 150 square feet (14 sq m), it was smaller than many modern closets.

could be started and finished during the early morning.

Thoreau also brought some cooking utensils, such as tongs, a frying pan, a kettle, a skillet, two knives and forks, three plates, a cup, a spoon, two jugs, a washbasin, and a dipper for water. He also kept his notebooks, some books, and writing instruments, but his time at Walden was decidedly simple. Early on, he kept three pieces of limestone on his desk for decoration, but threw them out when he realized they required daily dusting that distracted him from his work. When Thoreau was moving in, a friend offered him a mat to use as a carpet, but Thoreau turned it down, saying he could neither spare the space nor the time to shake it out.

Thoreau ate plainly at Walden Pond. In addition to the crops he had planted, he also sometimes ate wild nuts, berries, and game that he had caught, such as fish. Though at times a vegetarian, Thoreau occasionally lapsed back to eating meat. He once famously trapped, killed, and ate a woodchuck that had been destroying his garden. (The meat, he said, tasted surprisingly good.) He also took time

to experiment with bread recipes, which he mixed with lake water and cooked on a hot stone. He found **unleavened** bread to be the simplest to make. According to some stories, he once added raisins to his bread dough, and thereby invented raisin bread.

Thoreau's time at Walden proved extraordinarily productive. He finished his draft for *A Week on the Concord and Merrimack Rivers*, the book about the Thoreau brothers' sailing trip that Henry had wanted so desperately to complete, as well as some essays and lectures. When Concord residents learned of his experiment, they began asking him about his time there, how he lived, what his house was like, and if he was scared to live alone. Thoreau decided to respond to these inquiries by penning a series of lectures based on his notes and journal entries, which he later organized into a book-length manuscript entitled *Walden: or, Life in the Wood*s.

Economy

Thoreau's experiment at Walden Pond had a variety of goals. Foremost among them was his plan to live as simply as possible and thereby free himself from having to labor at tasks he did not want to do to earn a living. Thoreau summarized his theory this way: "I am convinced, both by faith and experience, that to maintain one's self on this earth is not a hardship but a pastime, if we will live simply and wisely … It is not necessary that a man should earn his living by the sweat of his brow unless he sweats easier than me."

Thoreau's theory of personal finance hinged on the fact that money is the rate of exchange between goods and a person's time: "[T]he cost of a thing is the amount of what I will call life which is required to be exchanged for it, immediately or in the long run." In modern economics, a person's wage is understood to be the amount of money a person charges their employers for his time—in other words, people sell their time to an employer, so that they may earn enough money to buy the things they want. In this sense, time has an inverse relationship to material possessions: the more one wants, the more time and freedom one must sacrifice to get it.

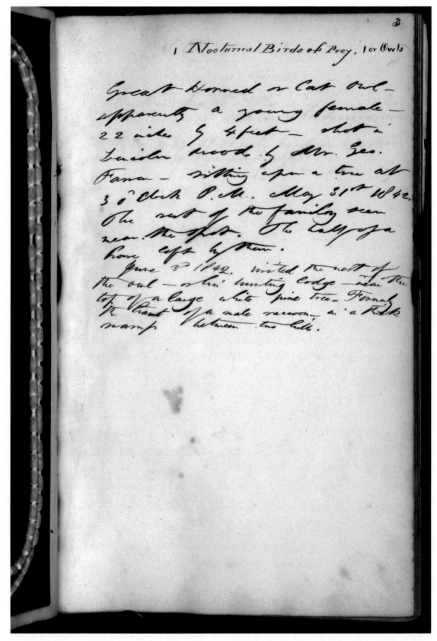

While he was working on the manuscript for *A Week on the Concord and Merrimack Rivers*, Thoreau also kept a journal documenting his experiences and observations at the pond. These notes eventually grew into *Walden: or, Life in the Woods*, his best-known work.

THOREAU,
THE WOODS BURNER

In the years since *Walden* was first published, Thoreau has inspired generations of environmental activists. His vision of simple living in nature in many ways proved that a person can live a comfortable, fulfilling life without all the excess and environmental degradation that accompanies industrialization and consumerism. However, as much as Thoreau was a lover of nature, one afternoon he was also responsible for destroying most of the remaining woodland in his hometown.

On April 30, 1844, Thoreau and his friend Edward Hoar took a rowboat to go fishing in the Sudbury River. They got a decent catch, which they hoped to make into a chowder. They stopped along the river and built a fire out of an old stump. "The earth was uncommonly dry," Thoreau later said, and the stump was covered in dried grass, which caught fire. Thoreau and Hoar tried to extinguish the fire by stomping on it, and then pounding it with a board from their boat, but they could do nothing to put it out.

As they sprinted back to Concord for help, Thoreau stopped to watch the progress of the **conflagration**, which ravaged most of the forest. The fire burned over 300 acres (121 ha) of woodland. A great deal of it was private property, and nearly all of it the last remaining parcels of untouched woodland in town, which was quickly shrinking due to deforestation as a result of the industrial revolution. The *Concord Freeman* newspaper estimated total damage at over $2,000 and criticized Thoreau for being thoughtless. Residents of Concord resented Thoreau for the damage and took to calling him the "Woods Burner."

Six years later, Thoreau recalled the event, saying, "Hitherto I had felt like a guilty person—nothing but shame and regret. But now I settled the matter with myself shortly. I said to myself, 'Who are these men who are said to be the owners of these woods, and how am I related to them? I have set fire to the forest, but I have done no wrong therein, and now it is as if the lightning had done it." Although he stated that he no longer felt remorseful for starting the forest fire, the fact that he was still thinking back on it six years later suggests otherwise.

To Thoreau, the way to personal freedom began, as his book *Walden* begins, with an examination of personal economy. The fewer things people could live with, the less time they had to spend to buy them, and, thus, the more time they could have to themselves.

Thoreau documented the financial aspects of his experiment in "Economy," the first chapter in *Walden*. Thoreau's simple lodging enabled him to live extremely frugally. As he wrote in "Economy," "my greatest skill has been to want but little." This personality trait would be the foundation for his success in Walden. Thoreau's tiny cabin itself cost precisely $28.125 (the third decimal place may seem odd to modern readers, but it highlights Thoreau's exacting attitude to personal finance). Perhaps his most wasteful building expense was nails, on which he spent $3.90, apparently because he could not always drive them properly. (When archaeologists in the 1940s excavated the site of Thoreau's cabin, they found the floor of his cellar littered with hundreds of bent nails. Had he managed to properly drive them, Thoreau could have saved much of the nearly four dollars he had spent replacing them.) His other living expenses were similarly modest. After 8 months living at Walden, Thoreau learned he had only spent $8.74 on food (27¢ per week), just over $8 on clothes, and $2 on fuel for his fire. Together with other necessities, Thoreau's first eight months of living expenses amounted to only about $60.

On the income side of his budget, Thoreau managed to feed himself as well as make a profit from his crops, which, true to his hypothesis, required only minimal upkeep. From the sale of his vegetables, Thoreau made forty dollars in profit over his first eight months. It's not a stretch to say that Thoreau would have recouped the entirety of his initial investment within his first year, and from then on could have made a profit on the sale of his crops.

To Thoreau, it was clear that the math sustained the reality of his experiment. Anyone, he argued, could live the way he did—that is, comfortably, with low overhead and modest profit gleaned from minimal labor. Indeed, Thoreau's way of living was accessible to even the most impoverished classes of American society at that time. Agricultural laborers in Massachusetts at the time made between $120 and $140 per year, and elsewhere, even the least paid laborers could expect to make about $50. Thoreau specifically directed the benefits of his experiment to students, whose scant budgets and meager incomes resembled Thoreau's, indicating that they, too, could set themselves up in a similar way. In fact, this is still the case. With the rising costs of college education, the amount the average student spends on a dorm room annually could purchase a mobile home. (It is important to keep in mind, however, that Thoreau did not have to worry about purchasing the land on which his property sat or the taxes that are associated with property ownership. If this had been the case, his margins at Walden would have been much tighter than they were.)

Thoreau was convinced that the source of individual's economic problems was unreflective consumption. According to Thoreau, "The mass of men lead lives of quiet desperation." For an idea of what he means by "mass of men," the passages prior to Thoreau's observation shed some light. Thoreau precedes this quote with a short but comprehensive catalogue of people whose lives are spent acquiring a surplus of transient wealth. In this catalogue, Thoreau includes those men of a higher class who have inherited a sizable amount of material with which to make a living, including a house, a field, and farming equipment. However, Thoreau also lists the poor, and blue-collar workers as well, who, unlike those who have inherited material, have a difficult time making a living.

Though these men represent wildly disparate incomes and levels of material "comfort," they are united in this quiet desperation, which is understood as mere survival without living. Thoreau writes that these men are nothing but machines, but unlike any other machine, they incessantly turn their wheels but arrive nowhere. Their lives are spent in servitude to another: the rich who have inherited great wealth must work hard at sustaining their extravagant lifestyles. Thoreau calls their "fortunes"—a house, a field, or even just tools—

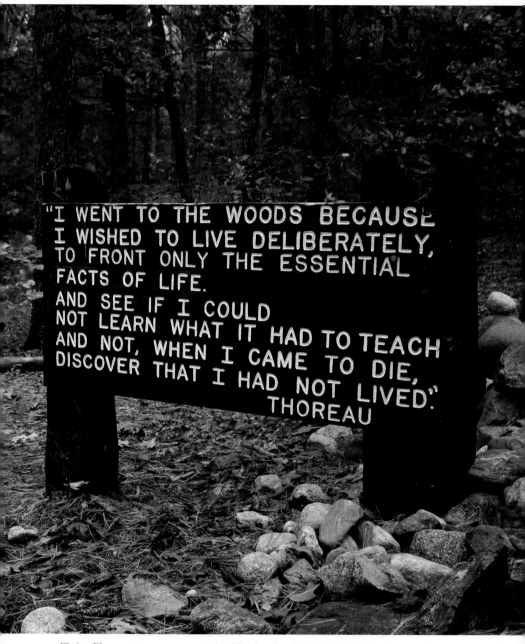

Today, Thoreau is commemorated at Walden Pond, which is a Massachusetts State Reservation and enjoys National Historic Landmark status.

"inherited encumbrances" that comprise a surfeit of production. Thoreau writes, "Why should they eat their sixty acres [24 ha], when man is condemned to eat only his peck of dirt?" Meanwhile, the poor who find it hard to live are subject to their creditors. Both groups are born into their social class and, modeling themselves on others of their same class, try to secure what little they have by the same means, disregarding what they need most.

Although it's easy to consider Thoreau's experiment to be antisocial, this isn't the case. While he did criticize the way in which the common man lived, he did not disavow society entirely. After all, his cabin at Walden was located along the main road from town and equidistant between a popular lake and the railroad. He often left a chair outside his cabin as an invitation to passersby, whom he only turned away when he was busy writing. He hosted visitors, both friends and strangers alike. Given this, it's clear that Thoreau wasn't inherently antisocial but rather desired a truer association between people.

Nature and Self Discovery

Freed from the necessity of laboring six days out of the week, Thoreau spent the rest of his time at Walden in the manner he preferred: waking at dawn, reading and writing in the morning, and hiking in the afternoons. Thoreau's experiment in living in nature was also a retreat for creative work, and the two informed one another. His task of writing *A Week* required quiet reflection about a trip he had taken in nature with his brother. Given the recent passing of his brother, the task of recalling happy memories in the midst of a reality of loss was emotionally draining for Thoreau. Fortunately, nature was both his subject and his source of spiritual renewal:

> We need the tonic of wildness … At the same time that we are earnest to explore and learn all things, we require that all things be mysterious and unexplorable,

that land and sea be indefinitely wild, unsurveyed, and unfathomed by us because unfathomable. We can never have enough of nature. We must be refreshed by the sight of inexhaustible vigor, vast and Titanic features, the sea-coast with its wrecks, the wilderness with its living and decaying trees, the thunder cloud, and the rain which lasts three weeks and produces freshets. We need to witness our own limits transgressed, and some life pasturing freely where we never wander.

The nature Thoreau found at Walden was not only an emotional salve but also a source of self-discovery. As a Transcendentalist, Thoreau believed that there was divinity within himself, and that he could learn everything he needed to learn about himself by experiencing the natural world around him. "Men esteem truth remote, in the outskirts of the system, behind the farthest star, before Adam and after the last man," Thoreau writes. "But all these times and places and occasions are now and here. God culminates in the present moment ... And we are enabled to apprehend at all what is sublime and noble only by the perpetual instilling and drenching of the reality which surrounds us." To Thoreau, salvation is not grasped at over a lifetime but found daily, if one is but willing to look for it. The goal should not be salvation at the end of life but actively seeking physical and spiritual renewal at the beginning of each day. In that way, *Walden* documents his self-actualization. Thoreau progresses from an economic being to a natural being to being itself.

CHAPTER FOUR

Resistance to Civil Government

Thoreau's cabin was not the only place he spent time in during the course of his experiment at Walden Pond. Thoreau also spent a night in prison. From his cabin to the confines of his Concord jail cell, Thoreau found himself in what may seem to outside observers as the polar opposite of his **naturalist** retreat. And yet, this imprisonment was practically as valuable to Thoreau as his liberation in nature, for both were deliberate actions in the interest of pursing his conscience.

One evening in late July 1846, Thoreau walked to Concord village to pick up shoes he had left at the cobbler's shop. While on his way there, a man named Sam Staples stopped him. Staples wore many hats, including the village constable, tax collector, and jailor. The reason for the stop this particular night was Thoreau's refusal to pay his poll

In July 1846, Thoreau spent a night in Concord Jail for refusing to pay his poll tax. Ironically, his prison cell likely boasted more space than his cabin at Walden.

tax. The poll tax administered by the state of Massachusetts was a tax **levied** on every male between the ages of twenty and seventy. In this way, it was like a citizenship tax, although not all the men who had to pay the tax were legally allowed to vote. During the conversation, Staples offered to pay Thoreau's tax himself, or at least to speak to the legislators and convince them to lower Thoreau's tax obligation. However, Thoreau did not simply neglect to pay his taxes; he consciously refused to do so on moral grounds. Staples informed Thoreau that if he did not pay his tax, Staples would soon arrest him and put him in prison. "As well now as any time, Sam," Thoreau responded, and so Staples took him to the Concord jail.

Thoreau and Taxes

This was not the first time Thoreau had taken a principled stand on taxation. In the mid-nineteenth century, in addition to the poll tax, Massachusetts also administered taxes on behalf of churches to raise money from their congregants. Thoreau's family had long been members of the First Parish Church and even owned a pew there. In 1840, the state sent Henry David Thoreau a church tax bill. At once, Thoreau went down to the town office and declared that he would not pay it. As with the poll tax, refusal to pay the church tax would result in imprisonment. Before it came to that, however, someone else paid Thoreau's tax for him. However, Thoreau would not let the matter remain undecided. He demanded that his name be removed from the church tax rolls and filed a statement with Concord's legislators that said, "Know by all men these presents, that I, Henry Thoreau, do not wish to be regarded as a member of any incorporated society which I have not joined." Thoreau was never again billed. (Furthermore, Thoreau noted during a review of the town's tax records that his name was documented as David H. Thoreau, which he had by this point unofficially changed to Henry David Thoreau. He argued successfully with the town clerk that his name be changed then and there.)

Then as in 1846, the reason for Thoreau's refusal was principled. In the case of the church tax, Thoreau did not find it just that he should be required to pay for membership in a community that he did not himself join. In July 1846, Thoreau's justification was based on his opposition to the federal government's policy on slavery and particularly its involvement in the budding conflict in the Southwest, which would become the Mexican-American War.

Slavery and the Mexican-American War

The Mexican-American War, as its name suggests, was a period of armed conflict between the United States and the Republic of Mexico, which at that time had only recently won independence from Spain as a result of revolution. The reasons for the United States' invasion of Mexico are multifaceted and inform one another. At the time, the United States was a well-organized republic of states, whereas the Mexican government was struggling to consolidate control over the large territory it had liberated from Spanish control. In the wake of the revolution, Mexico encouraged Americans to settle in their northern territory known as Texas. Many Americans flocked to the Southwest to claim parcels of land. However, within a decade, they came to resent Mexican rule. These American settlers waged a revolution against Mexico, declaring Texas an independent republic. In the United States, there was a push to incorporate the Texas Republic and its American settlers into the Union. To Mexico, doing so would have been an act of war.

The desire to admit Texas into the United States was part of a broader foreign policy that became known as **manifest destiny**, which was gaining widespread popularity. According to manifest destiny, it was not only America's right but its duty to expand from one end of the North American continent to the other, establishing an empire from the Atlantic to the Pacific Ocean and spreading American ideals of liberty and equality. Ironically, this drive meant America was free to dispose of preexisting inhabitants, including

Along with the nationalist policy of manifest destiny, many Americans, particularly in the South, supported the war with Mexico in the hopes of adding more slaveholding states to the nation.

Native tribes and Mexican settlers, and their lands in the territories west of the Mississippi River.

Between the United States' aggressive foreign policy and Mexico's political imbalance, which left it vulnerable to the possibility of invasion, the situation was ripe for war. In 1844, the American people elected James K. Polk as President. Polk had campaigned on national expansion, and he immediately went to work on acquiring Mexican territories. When negotiations to purchase the land from Mexico failed, the Mexican people's sense of indignation was inflamed. Under no circumstances would the United States seize Mexican land without a fight. In response, Polk sent General Zachary Taylor to the Rio Grande River, where the border between Mexico and the United States was disputed. Mexican and American troops clashed, causing Polk to announce that "Mexico … has invaded our territory and shed American blood on American soil." Congress rode the wave of popular support and declared war in 1846.

An important aspect of this American expansionist policy was the issue of slavery. Since its founding, the United States had been a slaveholding nation; however, not every state in the Union was a slaveholding state. Most slave states were located in the South, where many slave owners used slaves to work large tobacco and cotton plantations. Conversely, Northern states, with a climate that was largely unsuitable for such large-scale agricultural production, had transitioned into sophisticated industrial economies powered by machine manufacturing.

This difference in economic production caused a rift between Northern and Southern states, which deepened over time due, in large part, to America's desire to expand its borders. As the United States expanded, the question arose as to whether the new territories would be slaveholding states as in the South or free states as in the North. The answer to that question affected the balance of power at the national level. There was a fear among slaveholding states that the North would soon overtake them politically and use their influence to ultimately **abolish** slavery in the South, thereby overturning a supposed economically-crucial (and horrific) practice that had become a way of life. Fueled by this anxiety, many Southerners pushed for expansion into Mexican-held territories in the Southwest, where they thought new slaveholding states could be established to halt the influence of the free states.

Despite this **partisan** underpinning, the war in Mexico had wide public support. Although the standing American army at the start of the war numbered only several thousand men, some two hundred thousand civilians later volunteered to fight. Newspapers' coverage of the conflict increased public support in the United States against Mexico and cast the conflict in global, and even spiritual, terms.

Abolitionism

Although patriotic support for the Mexican-American War ran deep, not everyone in the United States supported it. Among the opponents to the war were a group of people known as abolitionists, who believed slavery was one of the United States' great moral failings and that the war, fought in part to spread slavery, was by extension reprehensible. Among those who opposed the war in Mexico was the well-known abolitionist William Lloyd Garrison, a senator from Illinois named Abraham Lincoln, and Henry David Thoreau.

Even among abolitionists, however, there were disputes as to how exactly to go about ending slavery. While united in their opposition to the institution, there were two conflicting views on how to do this. On the one hand, William Lloyd Garrison argued that there needed to be a reformation of society. Garrison and others accused the church, the government, and the media of defending slavery and advocated for the creation of large, aggressive antislavery societies. On the other hand, some abolitionists believed that the way to end slavery was the reformation of individuals themselves. Rather than wage a large-scale political revolution, these abolitionists argued that it was up to each individual to reform oneself and act according to one's own conscience. Naturally, this position appealed to Thoreau's own Transcendental philosophy of individual importance. Inspired to reform himself, Thoreau refused to pay his taxes on the grounds that doing so would implicitly support the war in general and slavery in particular, and therefore violate his conscience.

Thoreau's chance to make his moral objection to these taxes publicly and dramatically known did not come until July 1846, when Staples arrested him. Although Thoreau had refused to pay his poll tax for years, Staples simply chose to ignore Thoreau's protest during that time. Staples had a high opinion of Thoreau, despite being skeptical of the woodsman's Transcendental inclinations, and must have been content to leave the matter well enough alone. Why Staples decided to finally arrest Thoreau is uncertain. Some historians speculate that Staples was pressured to reconcile the books because he was about to give up his position as tax collector. On the other hand, the declaration of war against Mexico may have sparked patriotism in the village, and residents may have demanded that Thoreau perform his civic duty and pay the tax. In any event, the arrest was precipitated by several warnings. Thoreau did not heed them, nor did he change his habit of walking into town. At last, Staples decided he might as well arrest the tax evader.

Concord Jail

When Thoreau's mother got wind of her son's arrest, she rushed down to the Concord jail to learn the truth, then went home to share the news with the family. At some point in the night, somebody—most likely Thoreau's aunt, Maria—brought Thoreau's bail money to Sam Staples' house. Sam Staples was out, but his daughter told him about the package when he returned later. By this point, Staples had already removed his boots and was relaxing by the fire, with no intention of rousing himself again for the night. Staples said that it would be just as well for Thoreau to spend the night in jail.

"A PLEA FOR CAPT. JOHN BROWN"

"On Resistance to Civil Government" was not the only time Thoreau weighed in on the question of slavery during his lifetime. On October 30, 1859, Thoreau delivered "A Plea for Captain John Brown" to the residents of Concord in response to Brown's failed raid on Harper's Ferry.

On October 16, 1859, a Northern abolitionist named John Brown marched a small force of eighteen men into Harper's Ferry, Virginia; Virginia was, at the time, a slave state. The plan seemed doomed from the beginning. Brown had no planned escape route should things go south, and his "army," if they could be called that, was too small to maintain any substantial siege on the town. However, Brown hoped that his raid would inspire other abolitionists and enslaved communities throughout the South to take up arms and join the fight. Despite quickly capturing the town's armory, arsenal, and engine house, Brown failed to convince abolitionists and slaves to join him. Meanwhile, a militia had formed to defend the town. After exchanges of gunfire in which eight of Brown's men were killed, Brown and his remaining cohort retreated to the engine house. On October 18, Lieutenant Colonel Robert E. Lee marched federal troops from Washington, DC, to intercept Brown and his men. Brown was arrested and found guilty of treason and sentenced to hang on December 2.

Southerners were outraged, and many national newspapers made Brown out to be a fool. However, to some outspoken abolitionists such as Thoreau, Brown was exercising his right to affect change in the face of injustice. Echoing "On Resistance to Civil Government," Thoreau wrote, "Is it not possible that an individual may be right and a government wrong? Are laws to be enforced simply because they were made? Or declared by any number of men to be good, if they are *not* good?"

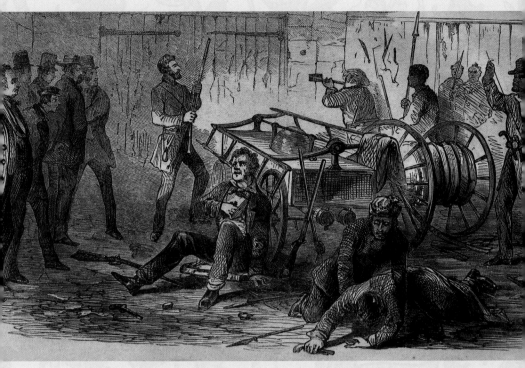

Abolitionist John Brown's failed raid at Harper's Ferry earned him the animosity of Southerners. Many in the North who supported abolition nevertheless considered him a fool. To Thoreau, however, Brown was a hero.

Elsewhere in "A Plea," Thoreau imbues Brown's raid with divine undertones. Like Thoreau himself had done on several occasions throughout his life, Brown endeavored to shape reality according to the way he saw it. In that way, Thoreau writes, Brown is an admirable Transcendentalist: "One writer says that Brown's peculiar monomania made him to be 'dreaded by the Missourians as a supernatural being.' Sure enough, a hero in the midst of us cowards is always so dreaded. He is just that thing. He shows himself superior to nature. He has a spark of divinity in him." Far from a fool, Brown was to Thoreau's mind the ideal all men should aspire to: a man so committed to his personal principles that he was willing to sacrifice himself to realize them.

This pamphlet from the 1830s demonstrates the growing support of abolitionism at the time, especially among Americans in the North. However, slavery would not be abolished until decades later.

Thoreau made the most of his time in prison. He occupied one of Concord jail's eighteen cells, which was nearly double the size of his cabin at Walden Pond. His cellmate, who was accused of **arson** and awaiting trial, told him that he was content to be there: after all, the man had his room and board paid for, and was allowed to leave each morning to work in the hayfields—a situation not very different from Thoreau's experiment in simplicity.

The following day, Staples went to the jail to release Thoreau. To the constable's surprise, Thoreau said he was not willing to leave. Staples said Thoreau was "as mad as the devil" that someone had paid his taxes on his behalf. But the point of Thoreau's imprisonment was to respect his conscience and dramatically draw attention to the cause of **abolitionism**—neither of which could be achieved through his early release. Staples told Thoreau, "Henry, if you will not go of your own accord I shall put you out, for you cannot stay here any longer." Thoreau **capitulated** and went back to the forest, stopping on his way to pick up his shoes from the cobbler.

"On Resistance to Civil Government"

Word of Thoreau's imprisonment spread quickly through the small village of Concord. Some of Thoreau's neighbors thought Thoreau's willful entrance into prison and his protests against his release were foolhardy. Concord resident James Garty, for example, at once acknowledged that Thoreau was a good man who "would pay every cent he owed to any man" and complained that "it wouldn't do to have everybody like him, or his way of thinking."

Among those who shared this opinion was Ralph Waldo Emerson. To Emerson, Thoreau's hardheadedness on the tax issue was irresponsible. In his journal, Emerson commented on Thoreau's time in prison, saying:

> The State is a poor, good beast who means the best: it means friendly. A poor cow who does well by you,—do

not grudge its hay ... As long as the state means you well, do not refuse your **pistareen**. You have a tottering cause: ninety parts of the pistareen it will spend for what you think also good: ten parts for mischief ... In the particular, it is worth considering that refusing payment of the state tax does not reach the evil so nearly as many other methods within your reach.

Emerson's first argument is that the state, for its shortcomings, means well. Despite Thoreau's personal objections to one particular aspect of the state's policies, it ought to be supported. On top of this, the likelihood that Thoreau's tax would have directly funded the fighting in Mexico was practically none. In fact, the absence of the funds in the public coffers has a greater potential to cause harm than if Thoreau paid his tax, as the tax went toward paying for public goods. Emerson concludes the entry by stating that Thoreau's trip to prison was dangerous: "The prison is one step to suicide." Time in prison in poor conditions and surrounded by criminals may have cost Emerson's friend his life.

Thoreau, in turn, took no notice of these criticisms and held true to his principles. One **apocryphal** story holds that Emerson visited Thoreau while he was in jail and asked him through the bars of the window what he was doing in there. Thoreau responded, "What are you doing out there?" (Although it is likely that Emerson directly asked Thoreau about his reasons for going to prison, there is hardly any evidence beyond historical repetition that the conversation happened at the prison, or that Thoreau responded in the way he did. It seems that the story of Emerson and Thoreau's conversation on opposite sides of the jailhouse bars is merely a legend born out of small-town gossip.)

Despite the sense of disappointment over Thoreau's actions among some of Concord's residents, many more were curious. Why would a man would refuse to pay his taxes and willingly go to prison, they wondered. Thoreau became both an oddity and a celebrity in town. As he would later do with the publication of *Walden*, Thoreau hoped to inform Concord's residents of the reasons for his decision by giving several lectures. On January 26, 1848, Thoreau delivered his lecture on "the relation of the individual to the State" at the Concord Lyceum. The audience was so receptive to what Thoreau had to say that he delivered the second half of his lecture again three weeks later.

The following year, a magazine publisher named Elizabeth Peabody wrote Thoreau asking for permission to publish his lecture in a periodical called *Aesthetic Papers*. At that time, Thoreau was busy correcting proofs for *A Week on the Concord and Merrimack Rivers*, but he sent a copy along within a week. Six weeks after that, Thoreau's essay, "On Resistance to Civil Government" (later known as "Civil Disobedience"), was published.

State Power vs. Individual Conscience

There is a tendency among Thoreau's disciples to imagine him as a **crotchety** recluse whose contempt for society led him to abandon it (as in *Walden*) and refuse participation in it (as in "On Resistance to Civil Government"). The former image of Thoreau is far from the truth; although living in relative seclusion at Walden Pond, Thoreau nevertheless desired to live just *outside* of society—far enough where he could find solitude, yet near enough that he could still enjoy the indisputable benefits of civilization.

Similarly, the interpretation that "On Resistance to Civil Government" is a treatise on anarchy achieved through tax evasion is also mistaken. As Thoreau himself wrote, "I ask, not at once no government, but at once a better government. Let every man make known what kind of government would command his respect, and that will be one step toward obtaining it." Although the catalyst for Thoreau's essay on disobeying the state was his imprisonment for refusing to pay his taxes, that is far from the central point of "On

Resistance to Civil Government." While his neighbors and colleagues may have disapproved of Thoreau's refusal to pay his poll tax, it was merely a protest, a conscious action based on underlying principles.

According to "On Resistance to Civil Government," there are at the same time two compelling forces in a person's life: the power of the state and that person's individual conscience, which occasionally come into conflict. For practically his entire life, Thoreau's core principle was the sanctity of the individual person: one's truth might as well be the truth of the entire world, for it is truth enough for oneself. Therefore, when the state and conscience come into conflict, conscience will—and must—win out.

For one, Thoreau writes, government is corruptible. While the United States' **democratic republic** may derive its powers from the consent of the governed, it is just as susceptible to tyranny as any other form of government. According to Thoreau, "This American government—what is it but a tradition, though a recent one, endeavoring to transmit itself unimpaired to posterity, but each instant losing some if its integrity? It has not the vitality and face of a single living man; for a single man can bend it to his will."

In the case of democracy, Thoreau states that the more likely scenario is majority rule:

> But a government in which the majority rule in all cases can not be based on justice, even as far as men understand it. Can there not be a government in which the majorities do not virtually decide right and wrong, but conscience?—in which majorities decide only those questions to which the rule of expediency is applicable? Must the citizen ever for a moment, or in the least degree, resign his conscience to the legislator? Why has every man a conscience then? I think that we should be men first, and subjects afterward. It is not desirable to cultivate a respect for the law, so much as for the right.

The only obligation which I have a right to assume is to do at any time what I think is right.

The problem with majority rule is that it leaves minorities—even a minority of one, as Thoreau—out in the cold. Without a means of realizing their conscience, they are pressured by the state into rejecting the very thing that makes them individuals. To Thoreau, that scenario is unacceptable.

Throughout history, as Thoreau writes, there have been those who have precisely made that individual sacrifice, becoming "machines" in the process. However, there are also those who choose the opposite: "A very few [men]—as heroes, patriots, martyrs, reformers in the great sense, and men—serve the state with their consciences also, and so necessarily resist it for the most part; and they are commonly treated as enemies by it." In these cases, the individual faces majority disapproval, but are often vindicated with time.

In Thoreau's ringing conclusion, he writes that the best government will be one that respects and acts according to men's consciences. However, that state will never be achieved if men like himself are forced to behave in ways counter to their consciences.

> There will never be a really free and enlightened State until the State comes to recognize the individual as a higher and independent power, from which its own power and authority are derived, and treats him accordingly. I please myself with imagining a State at last which can afford to be just to all men, and to treat the individual with respect as a neighbor; which even would not think it inconsistent with its own repose if a few were to live aloof from it, not meddling with it, nor embraced by it, who fulfilled all the duties of neighbors and fellow men. A State which bore this kind of fruit, and suffered it to drop off as fast as it ripened, would prepare the way for

a still more perfect and glorious State, which I have also imagined, but not yet anywhere seen.

To Thoreau, his refusal to pay his taxes did not mean that he did not want to participate in the political process; rather, doing so was precisely his way of participating. To Thoreau, participation in a government, even passive participation such as through paying taxes, communicates one's opinion of the way things are. This principle is actually essential to the democratic process, which is based on the consent of the governed. If, for example, one is dissatisfied with behavior of their elected officials, they may either choose not to vote or else vote for an opposing candidate.

When faced with events and policies that run counter to one's conscience, it is not only a right but an obligation to express one's disapproval and to halt one's compliance with injustice. In the same way a revolutionary might take up arms against a corrupt state, Thoreau chose to demonstrate his dissatisfaction with his government peacefully through his economic power. In that way, he was making a statement about the kind of government he wanted, one that did not wage war on neighboring countries for the sake of national expansion and, by extension, the expansion of slavery.

The Legacy of "On Resistance to Civil Government"

Thoreau's essay went largely unnoticed when it was first published. For one, *Aesthetic Papers* itself had a small circulation, and critics who took the time to read it were more concerned with other articles written by Ralph Waldo Emerson and Nathaniel Hawthorne, who were more famous at the time. A few of the essay's more forceful paragraphs were copied into the London-based magazine *People's Review*, but otherwise nothing immediately came of it.

In 1866, four years after Thoreau's death, the essay was published again as part of his book *A Yankee in Canada, with Anti-Slavery and*

Reform Papers. In this collection, it was renamed "Civil Disobedience," which has become the much more popular title of the two. Published a year after the Civil War and President Lincoln's Emancipation Proclamation, which freed the slaves in rebelling states, it would have seemed that there was no longer a need for Thoreau's paper recounting his reasons for going to prison. However, with this new chapter in the United States' history, there was renewed interest in his belief that individual conscience weighs supreme in the face of oppression at the hands of a majority government. Over time, the essay came to be seen less as the work of a half-rate hermit who spent a night in prison for not paying his taxes. Today, it is widely taught to students of both history and literature as one of America's foundational texts on human freedom.

Although Thoreau did not live to see the importance that his work would hold for future generations, he did understand that his most important role was to educate others on the importance of conscientious objection. He wrote: "I have never declined paying the highway tax, because I am desirous of being a good neighbor as I am of being a bad subject; and as for supporting schools, I am doing my part to educate my fellow countrymen now."

CHAPTER FIVE

Trials and Publications

I n the years after his experiment at Walden Pond, Thoreau turned his attention toward publishing. When he left his cabin in 1847, he had completed a manuscript of *A Week on the Concord and Merrimack Rivers*, which he hoped to publish, as well as copious notes and journal entries that would later serve as the foundation for *Walden: or, Life in the Woods*. Since the primary reason for Thoreau's experiment in simple living in the woods was to find the solitude and time he needed to write *A Week*, its publication naturally took precedence in Thoreau's mind.

A Week

In 1845, Evert Duyckinck of the Wiley & Putnam publishing house approached Nathaniel Hawthorne about the possibility

Thoreau found limited success publishing his works on nature during his lifetime. In the decades after his death, however, he would earn recognition as one of the greatest American writers of all time.

of launching a new series called "American Books." At that time, British publishers printing books by British authors dominated the American literary market, and Duyckinck hoped American Books would expand homegrown literature within the United States. In addition to asking Hawthorne if he might contribute a book to the project, Duyckinck also asked if Hawthorne knew of any promising young writers. Hawthorne, who had lived for a time in Concord, immediately recommended Thoreau. Two years later, on March 28, 1847, Thoreau submitted his manuscript of *A Week* to Duyckinck.

Duyckinck and his bosses at Wiley & Putnam had a favorable view of *A Week* and wrote to its author that they would be happy to publish it—with one catch: Thoreau would have to publish at his own expense. Then as now, publishing a book is a gamble—it is never clear if it will be well received by the public—but publishing a book on one's own dime only raises the stakes. Thoreau's friend Bronson Alcott assured him that the book would be a success, though: "The book is purely American, fragrant with the life of New England woods and streams, and could have been rwitten nowhere else." Thoreau's closest friend Emerson joined Alcott in praising the book and encouraging Thoreau to publish, though ideally with another publishing house that would offer a more favorable agreement.

After a few rounds of submissions to publishers around the country, Thoreau settled on Boston-based James Munroe & Co., who agreed to print *A Week*. After some negotiation, they agreed that Thoreau would pay the costs of publishing the book gradually out of its sales with the understanding that he would eventually pay them the full amount. They also agreed to publish *Walden*, which Thoreau was hard at work on, in the future.

A Week was published on May 30. Despite the minor publicity Thoreau's publisher invested in the book, comprising only brief notes in a magazine and a local newspaper, the book nevertheless received widespread attention and garnered generally favorable reviews. However, the book was a commercial **flop**. When booksellers returned their unsold copies (which were numerous) to the publisher, the publisher in turn gave the copies to its author. In October 1853, Thoreau wrote in his journal that he received 706 copies out of an edition of 1,000. "They are something more substantial than fame," Thoreau wrote with the sense of humor needed by a writer in such a situation, "as my back knows, which has borne them up two flights of stairs to a place similar to that which they trace their origin … I now have a library of nearly nine hundred volumes, over seven hundred of which I wrote myself."

The failure of *A Week* put Thoreau deeply in debt. He tried to make enough money to cover his obligations to James Munroe & Co. by manufacturing one thousand dollars' worth of pencils at his father's factory. Unfortunately for Thoreau, when he went to New York to sell them, the market was glutted, and he sold his stock at a loss. A month later, he managed to scrape together the final payment to his publisher. All told, his payments totaled $290, this for a book that only netted him $15 in profit. Perhaps worse, Munroe & Co. refused to publish *Walden* in the face of *A Week*'s poor showing.

Although those in town who disliked Thoreau chose to use his misfortune as an opportunity to deride him, Thoreau chose to take the event as a teaching moment. Looking to improve his writing, he noted in his journal:

> My faults are:—
> Paradoxes,—saying just the opposite,—a style which may be imitated.
> Ingenious.
> Playing with words,—getting the laugh,—not always simple, strong, and broad.
> Using current phrases and maxims, when I should speak for myself.
> Not always earnest.
> "In short," "in fact," "alas!" etc.
> Want of conciseness.

Undeterred by *A Week*'s financial shortcoming, Thoreau continued to look for a publisher for *Walden* while pursuing other literary projects. He began lecturing again and found some success outside of Concord. Contrary to what some later scholars have written of Thoreau, that they considered him to be a poor public speaker too often caught up with navel-gazing, Thoreau proved an engaging and entertaining lecturer. Having weathered a commercial disaster, Thoreau was keen to make his audiences laugh. A review in the *Salem Observer* described Thoreau's lecture on "Economy" as demonstrating "exquisite humor." It continued to state that his "interspersed observations, speculations, and suggestions upon dress, fashions, food, dwellings, furniture, etc., etc., sufficiently queer to keep the audience in almost constant mirth ... The performance has created 'quite a sensation' amongst the Lyceum goers." In the Worcester *Palladium*, Thoreau's schoolmate from Harvard, H. G. O. Blake, described his lecture there as "witty, sarcastic, and amusing."

Cape Cod

In October 1849, Thoreau departed from Concord for a trip to Cape Cod. Located in the southeastern part of Massachusetts, Cape Cod is a peninsula that extends out and up into the Atlantic Ocean. Today, it is a popular destination for families on summer holidays as well as retirees, who flock to the peninsula's peaceful sandy shores. However, Cape Cod in Thoreau's time was very different from the Cape Cod of today. Back then, the Cape was home to a hardy lot of fishermen, mariners, and salvagers known as "wreckers," who scavenged the remains of shipwrecks that washed ashore looking for anything of value. (It seems shipwrecks were so common in the region that these wreckers could make a decent living.) These residents constantly battled the bad weather endemic to the region.

When Thoreau chose his excursion to Cape Cod as the subject of his next book, he must have known that it would stir up some waves. In the mid-1800s, books known as travelogues, which documented the writer's experiences abroad, were becoming a popular form. These narratives were almost always leisurely accounts of the writer exploring exotic locales, meant to entice the reader with aesthetically pleasing descriptions. In other words, travelogues were what we might call "beach reading."

Thoreau's *Cape Cod* veers decidedly away from that form. His subject matter—the windblown residents and salt-caked shores of Cape Cod—are a far cry from the idyllic pastures and scenic vistas of conventional travelogues. Likewise is his treatment of the material. With his reliance on facts and oral history, coupled with what is at times cold description, Thoreau's *Cape Cod* reads more like a newspaper article than a flight of fancy. Nowhere in the book is this better illustrated than the opening, where Thoreau describes a beach covered not with sunbathers but with bodies:

> The brig *St. John*, from Galway, Ireland, laden with emigrants, was wrecked on Sunday morning; it was now Tuesday morning, and the sea was still breaking violently on the rocks. There were eighteen or twenty of the same large boxes [coffins] that I have mentioned, lying on a green hill-side, a few rods from the water, and surrounded by a crowd. The bodies which have been recovered, twenty-seven or eight in all, had been collected there. Some were rapidly nailing down the lids, others were carrying the boxes away, and others were lifting the lids, which were yet loose, and peeping under the cloths, for each body, with such rags as still adhered to it, was covered loosely with a white sheet. I witnessed no signs of grief, but there was a sober despatch of business which was affecting. One man was seeking to identify a particular body, and one undertaker or carpenter was calling to another to know in what box a certain child was put.

Tens of thousands of Irish immigrants boarded so-called coffin ships to escape the Great Hunger. However, conditions aboard the overcrowded, dirty, diseased ships was hardly an improvement. Many died en route to their destination due to disease, not to mention those who died in shipwrecks.

The *St. John* was one of the so-called "**coffin ships**" that were packed full of immigrants from Ireland hoping to escape what they called *an Gorta Mór*—the Great Hunger. In the mid-1800s, Ireland was suffering through a deadly famine brought on by a blight that affected the potato crops. By this point, potatoes had become the primary staple of the Irish commoner's diet. As a result, more than a million Irish people died, and 1.6 million more fled to the United States in search of refuge. Those who survived the trip were met with institutional discrimination. Many businesses refused to hire Irish laborers, forcing them to work as nannies, janitors, gardeners, and unskilled laborers. In the words of Boston Mayor Theodore Lyman, many Americans felt that the Irish who arrived in America were "a race that will never be infused into our own, but on the contrary will remain distinct and hostile."

In writing *Cape Cod*, Thoreau looked to subvert a popular form to undermine popular American notions, especially those associated with manifest destiny. As the United States was looking westward toward what it believed to be its birthright, Thoreau traveled east, to the shores of the Atlantic. In describing the carnage as a result of the *St. John*, Thoreau pointed to the contradiction at play in American politics: On the one hand, manifest destiny promised to bring superior American values and liberties to the West; yet in one of the original thirteen colonies, on the shores of Cape Cod, the bodies of immigrants seeking refuge went unacknowledged.

If the point was not fully conveyed, Thoreau highlighted his criticism of American society with his contradictory descriptions of the wreckers. The wreckers were individualists seeking out an existence in a hard place at the same time they were profit-hungry parasites, like crabs scuttling out of their holes in the sand to pick apart a dead sea creature. "But are we not all wreckers," Thoreau asked, "contriving that one treasure may be washed up on our beach, that we may secure it, and do we not infer the habits of these Nauset and Barnegat wreckers, from the common modes of getting a living?"

The famine in Ireland hit hardest commoners, who depended on the potato as a dietary staple. An estimated one million people died during the Great Hunger.

In many ways, *Cape Cod* stands in opposition to *Walden*. Whereas *Walden* optimistically celebrates the capability of the individual to be daily renewed in and by nature, *Cape Cod* demonstrates the hostility nature can throw at man. Thoreau characterized the land itself as taking a hostile shape, describing the peninsula as the arm of a boxer. The sea, meanwhile, pummels the people liberally. "As I looked over the water," Thoreau wrote, "I saw the isles rapidly wasting away, the sea nibbling voraciously at the continent, the sprinting arch of a hill suddenly interrupted, as at Point Alderton,—what botanists might call premorse [describing something bitten off],—showing, by its curve against the sky, how much space it must have occupied, where now was water only."

Economy (Again)

Although writing was the only career Thoreau had wanted, in his later years he needed to pursue other means to earn a living, which writing could not do for him. Fortunately for Thoreau, he found a job that could satisfy both his need to make money and his desire to be in nature: **surveying**. Although Thoreau continued to write extensively in his journal as well as to pen some essays in the later years of his life, his primary occupation became surveying.

Thoreau made a name for himself once word of his skill in marking out the land got around. Despite his reputation as a hermit, Thoreau was commissioned for a variety of surveying projects both in Concord and around the Northeast. He surveyed roads, including a street for a railroad company that led to a depot, lots for townhouses for realtors, and even the Concord courthouse. In 1856, Thoreau was hired to survey a community based in New Jersey. Thoreau's reputation as a scrupulous surveyor even led Concord landowner Charles Bartlett to hire him to settle a land dispute between Bartlett and Emerson. Bartlett knew of Thoreau's relationship with Emerson, yet trusted him to resolve the dispute without bias.

Surveying helped Thoreau earn what many of his neighbors may have considered a more honest living. Nevertheless, he maintained his Transcendentalist views, though he had in many ways returned to the ordinary workaday world. When the United States was again thrust into an economic depression in 1857 and banks began to fail, Thoreau noted:

> The merchants and company have long laughed at transcendentalism, higher laws, etc., crying "None of your moonshine," as if they were anchored to something not only definite, but sure and permanent. If there was any institution which was presumed to rest on a solid and secure basis, and more than any other represented this boasted common sense, prudence, and practical talent, it was the bank; and now those very banks are found to be mere reeds shaken by the wind. Scarcely one in the land has kept its promise … But there is the moonshine still, serene, beneficent, and unchanged. Hard times, I say,

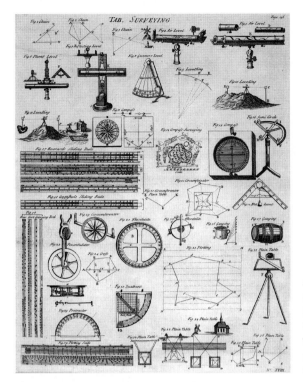

A table of common surveying tools. Thoreau's success in surveying depended less on his skill with such tools as much as his years of experience exploring nature.

have this value, among others, that they show us what such promises are worth,—where the sure banks are.

While pursuing a living as a surveyor, Thoreau never lost sight of his habits and his ideas. Although his ability to work on larger writing projects suffered, Thoreau continued to assemble notes and observations in his journals. The time he spent surveying sometimes halted his regular journal entries, which ceased for days at a time, but more often this work informed his journal. While laying out a road for a real estate developer, for example, Thoreau took notes in pencil on the field and later transcribed his comments in ink for his journal. As a man of nature, the fact that he could spend his days outdoors helped realize the dream he had set out in *Walden*, even though he had long since left the pond.

CHAPTER SIX

Later Life and Legacy

I n the later years of Thoreau's life, his tuberculosis, which he had largely kept at bay as a result of his habit of strenuous outdoor exercise and activities, started to catch up with him. He still managed to continue his work surveying, reading, writing, and publishing, and he took his walks in nature whenever he could manage, but his energy was severely affected as a result of the creeping illness in his lungs. During this time, Thoreau grew a beard, which he left almost completely untrimmed, as a means of combatting the colds that exacerbated his illness. To many, he seemed like a mossy stump of a man. His strength waned as he lost his appetite, and his physical appearance became frailer.

This ambrotype (a type of photograph) of Thoreau was taken in 1861, less than a year before his death.

Friends of Thoreau became increasingly concerned for his health. In 1860, Daniel Ricketson sent several letters inquiring into his friend's health. These went without reply until the late summer of 1861, when Thoreau said he would visit Ricketson at his home in New Bedford, Massachusetts, which was only a short walk from Concord. Though encouraged by Thoreau's visit, Ricketson commented,

> In relation to my friend Thoreau's health, my impression is that his case is a very critical one as to recovery; he has a bad cough and expectorates a good deal, is emaciated considerably, his spirits, however, appear as good as usual, his appetite good. Unless some favorable symptom shows itself too soon I fear he will gradually decline.

During this time, Ricketson encouraged Thoreau to have his picture taken with a local ambrotypist. It would be the last likeness of Thoreau left to posterity.

Thoreau's health briefly rallied in October 1861. The Hoar family offered him the use of their horse and wagon, and he went on near-daily horseback rides through the Concord woods. Many thought that, despite a persistent and violent cough, Thoreau's improvement was promising. However, whatever ground he had gained quickly vanished as the cold and wet winter set in. On November 3, Thoreau made what would be his last entry in his journal: "All this is perfectly distinct to an observant eye, and yet could easily pass unnoticed by most."

In the last months of his life, Thoreau continued to receive visitors. Each of them commented on the contradictory man they had found in Thoreau: though clearly suffering from a debilitating disease, Thoreau neither slouched nor exhibited any emotional turmoil. Though his fate was all but sealed, he continued to speak congenially with his friends, albeit with difficulty. In a letter to Myron Benton, a poet from Leedsville, New York, Thoreau wrote, "I *suppose* that I have not many months to live; but, of course, I know nothing about it. I may add that I am enjoying existence as much as ever, and regret nothing."

By the spring of 1862, Thoreau's life was clearly at an end, but he refused to abandon his love of nature. He tried in vain to scrape the frost from the window as he lay in bed, saying, "I cannot even see out-doors." He took pleasure in seeing his sister Sophia, who had by this point become his nurse, and asked her to open the doors to his room so that he could look out into her conservatory. And through this, he did not lose his sense of humor.

On May 6, 1862, around seven o'clock, Thoreau grew restless in his sickbed and asked to be moved. He had been dictating his notes for a series of new papers about the Maine Woods to Sophia for weeks. With his last breaths, his thoughts turned back to his writing, and he resumed dictating again as he slipped out of consciousness. At nine o'clock that night, he died. Sophia said, "I feel as if something very beautiful had happened—not death."

Thoreau's Legacy

Thoreau's influence went largely unacknowledged for a century after his death. On the one hand, many literary critics considered his work to be derivative of his mentor Ralph Waldo Emerson's work. Coupled with his struggle to find a market for his books, many people abandoned Thoreau's work in favor of other contemporary America writers who had greater success, including Emerson and Nathaniel Hawthorne. Nevertheless, Thoreau's sister Sophia diligently copied, organized, and preserved his published books and unpublished manuscripts and journal entries. This labor of love proved invaluable for modern readers and, today, Thoreau's legacy is far-reaching.

There are few areas of modern life that have not been touched in some way by Thoreau. *Walden*, once widely thought to be penned by an imitative hack, has since been translated into over a dozen languages and is required reading in practically every early American literature class in the United States. It has inspired generations of

Thoreau's writings inspired countless generations of environmental activists, including John Muir, who in 1903 took President Theodore Roosevelt to Yosemite Valley. Roosevelt was so inspired by the natural grandeur of Yosemite that he used his executive power to preserve many of America's natural landmarks.

environmental conservationists and activists, writers, philosophers, and those merely looking to simplify their lives. Many of America's most prominent environmental conservation organizations owe their charters in large part to Thoreau's work. In 1896, the first Audubon Society formed in Massachusetts with the mission to preserve the native birds that had captivated Thoreau throughout his life. In the Pacific, renowned conservationist John Muir took President Theodore Roosevelt on a camping trip to Yosemite Valley in California, which was threatened by overgrazing and expansive logging operations. Roosevelt was so inspired by the landscape and Muir's passion, which had been influenced in many ways by Thoreau, that he instituted the National Forest Service to preserve the United States' most irreplaceable natural treasures.

Thoreau's legacy also extends to the political. "On Resistance to Civil Government," known more popularly today as "Civil Disobedience" has appealed to some of history's greatest political activists. In the early twentieth century, Mahatma Gandhi led a movement founded on peaceful resistance to the oppressive British government in South Africa and India. Known as *Satyagraha*, Gandhi's passive resistance was directly inspired by Thoreau. Gandhi read "Civil Disobedience" in an 1866 anthology of Thoreau's writings and considered the English term "civil disobedience" to be a perfect translation of the Indian *Satyagraha*, granting Thoreau full credit for the movement.

Thoreau also inspired the twentieth-century civil rights activist Dr. Martin Luther King Jr. Like Gandhi, Dr. King organized peaceful resistance to oppressive government—in this case, the United States government, which had in the decades following the Civil War and the abolition of slavery allowed institutional racism to continue in the South. Like Thoreau, King was sent to jail, in his case in Birmingham, Alabama, after organizing a protest march despite an injunction from a federal judge prohibiting parading, boycotting, trespassing, and picketing. There, King penned his famous "Letters from a Birmingham Jail," in which he encourages his followers to continue their nonviolent resistance. Echoing Thoreau, King writes, "One has not only a legal but a moral responsibility to obey just laws. Conversely, one has a moral responsibility to disobey unjust laws." Gandhi and King have gone on to inspire countless revolutionaries and peaceful resisters, but they, in turn, found their original inspiration in Thoreau, who sought not to abolish government through passive resistance but to improve it. Indeed, Thoreau, Gandhi, and King's political actions are responsible for creating more just laws around the world.

Turning to the Old

Thoreau's influence is global, which is ironic, given that Thoreau hardly traveled during his life and then only within the northeastern part of the United States and briefly in Canada. Even when away, his internal compass always directed him back to Concord. Responsible for universal notions about simplicity, conservation, and political improvement through passive resistance that have appealed throughout time, Thoreau coined most of these ideas within the secluded woods outside of a small town with only two thousand residents. There he sought to understand his life through experiencing natural truths, because in those natural truths lie greater spiritual truths. Years after his death, it's obvious that the spiritual truths Thoreau discovered in the small woodland outside of his town have universal significance.

Thoreau's daily walks in the woods granted him an encyclopedic knowledge of his surroundings. He knew every rock and brook, every tree and stump, and every creature as if they were his friends. He used to delight the children of Concord with birdsongs, and he had a reputation for being unable to walk past a berry without plucking it. His neighbors often criticized Thoreau for his eccentricities. Even his friends poked fun at his boundless curiosity. To them he replied, "What else is there in life?" His response was not rhetorical; it was a challenge to others that reverberates and will continue to reverberate throughout time.

CHRONOLOGY

1817 Henry Thoreau is born in Concord, Massachusetts on July 12 to John Thoreau and Cynthia Dunbar Thoreau.

1821 Thoreau's father, John Thoreau, enters into a pencil-making business with his brother-in-law Charles Dunbar, who discovered a graphite deposit in New Hampshire.

1828–1833 Thoreau attends Concord Academy.

1833–1837 Thoreau attends Harvard College.

1834 A student in Professor Dunkin's class at Harvard displays open insubordination during a recitation on May 19, leading to the "Dunkin Rebellion" in which students destroyed College property and defaced effigies of Harvard's president Josiah Quincy.

1836 Thoreau is forced to temporarily withdraw from Harvard during the spring semester due to illness (tuberculosis).

1837 Thoreau twice withdraws *Nature* by Ralph Waldo Emerson from the Harvard Library during the spring semester; on August 30, Thoreau graduates from Harvard with a high enough class rank to participate in a commencement address; in the fall, Thoreau resigns from his position as schoolteacher at Concord Center School after being told to physically abuse misbehaving students; he changes his name from David Henry Thoreau (his christened name) to Henry David Thoreau; Thoreau strikes up a relationship with Ralph Waldo Emerson, a Concord intellectual, writer, and lecturer; on October 22, he starts a journal that he will regularly keep for the rest of his life, writing over 2,000,000 words and 7,000 printed pages of material; he joins the Hedge Club, a meeting of New England-based Transcendentalists.

1838–1841 Thoreau and his brother John operate Concord Academy, a private school.

1839 Thoreau and John depart on a boating trip on the Concord and Merrimack Rivers, which would serve as the inspiration behind his first book, *A Week on the Concord and Merrimack Rivers*.

1841–1843 Thoreau lives with Ralph Waldo Emerson and his family in Concord.

1842 Thoreau's brother John dies after contracting tetanus from cutting himself with a shaving razor.

1843 Thoreau moves to Staten Island, New York, where he tutors Emerson's nephew.

1844 Thoreau and Edward Hoar accidentally start a forest fire on April 30, which burned nearly 300 acres (121 ha) of Concord forests.

1845–1847 Thoreau moves into a one-room cabin on Emerson's land at Walden Pond; writes the bulk of a manuscript for *A Week on the Concord and Merrimack Rivers*.

1846 US president James K. Polk, elected on a campaign of national expansion, sends a representative to Mexico to negotiate the purchase of Mexican-held territory in the Southwest. Negotiations fail, and Polk sends an armed military force to disputed territory along the Rio Grande. After skirmishes with Mexican forces, the United States declares war.

1848 Thoreau is arrested in July for neglecting to pay his poll tax in protest of the Mexican-American War and spends a night in the Concord jail; after this, Thoreau begins lecturing professionally.

1849 Thoreau publishes *A Week on the Concord and Merrimack Rivers* and "On Resistance to Civil Government," an essay inspired by his night in the Concord jail; Thoreau's older sister Helen dies of tuberculosis.

1849–1850 Thoreau makes several trips to Cape Cod and another to Quebec, Canada.

1854 Publishes *Walden: or, Life in the Woods*.

1856 Surveys an organized community at Eagleswood, New Jersey.

1859 Between October 16 and 18, militant abolitionist John Brown leads a small army in an assault on Harper's Ferry, Virginia, in the hopes of sparking a large-scale slave insurrection. Brown captures the town's armory, arsenal, and engine house, but fails to inspire slaves to rebel. Brown is captured and sentenced to death by hanging in December. Father John Thoreau dies this year, and Thoreau delivers "A Plea for Capt. John Brown" to the Concord Lyceum.

1862 Thoreau dies in Concord of tuberculosis on May 6.

GLOSSARY

abolitionism The movement toward ending slavery.

apocryphal Describing a story of questionable accuracy or authenticity though widely circulated as true.

arson The crime of deliberately setting fire to a person's property.

capitulate To stop resisting a demand.

christened The act of admitting a baby into Christianity by giving him or her a Christian name at baptism.

classics A field of study including Latin and Greek literature, history, and philosophy.

coffin ship One of a number of overcrowded sailing ships that carried Irish immigrants fleeing from the potato famine of the nineteenth century; known for having appallingly high mortality rates.

commonplace book A notebook in which quotes from other books are copied for later use.

conflagration A fire that destroys a large amount of land and property.

cord A measure of wood equal to 4 feet (1.2 meters) by 4 feet (1.2 m) by 8 feet (2.4 m) of stacked split wood, or roughly fifty trees.

corporal punishment Physical punishment, such as caning.

credit The ability of a consumer to obtain goods or services before tendering payment through loans.

creditor Someone who loans money.

crotchety Irritable.

culling To reduce the population by selective slaughter.

democratic republic A form of government, as in the United States, in which citizens elect representatives to represent their interests and pass and enforce laws.

effigy A rough model of a person made to be destroyed in protest.

Enlightenment A philosophical movement in the seventeenth and eighteenth centuries and centered primarily in Western Europe that emphasized knowledge through individual human reason instead of relying on long-held tradition.

exorbitant Unreasonably expensive or excessive.

flop A total failure.

homogenous Of the same kind.

levy To impose something, such as a tax.

lyceum movement A movement in nineteenth-century America in which public auditoriums were constructed to facilitate lectures and debates on a variety of political, moral, and scientific topics.

malaise A general feeling of discomfort or uneasiness.

manifest destiny A policy of national expansion in the United States that believed it was the country's right and obligation to expand from one side of North America to the other based on a notion of the superiority of American values.

naturalist An expert in natural history.

partisan A firm adherent to a party, faction, cause, or person.

pistareen A Spanish coin used in America up until the eighteenth century whose stated value was above that of the materials it contained, making it debased; used to describe a small amount of money; a pittance.

plumbago An ore containing lead and suitable for pencils; graphite.

prototypical Describing the first or original version of something.

Romanticism A movement in arts and literature from the eighteenth and nineteenth centuries that was characterized by an appreciation for natural beauty, emphasis on personal experience of emotion over reason, and examination of the self and human personality.

slurry A mixture of liquid and fine particles, such as water and sand.

supplant To take the place of someone or something.

surveying To examine and record the features of a landscape for the purpose of mapping or building on that area.

teamster A driver of a team of animals.

tetanus A bacterial disease characterized by rigidity of certain muscles and involuntary spasms of muscles; also known as lockjaw.

Transcendentalism An American literary and philosophical movement characterized by a belief in the unity of creation, innate human goodness expressed through conscience, and the importance of personal insight over reason.

tuberculosis An infectious bacterial disease characterized by the spread of growths in tissues, especially in the lungs.

Unitarianism A religious belief growing out of Enlightenment reason that maintained the unity of God over the more orthodox belief in a Holy Trinity.

unleavened Bread made without yeast, the ingredient that causes bread dough to rise.

SOURCES

INTRODUCTION

pg. 5: U.S. Bureau of the Census. "Median and Average Square Feet of Floor Area in New Single-Family Houses Completed by Location," www.census.gov/const/C25Ann/sftotalmedavgsqft.pdf.

pg. 5: InvestorPlace. "Report: Average American is $225,238 in Debt." investorplace.com/2013/09/report-average-american-in-debt-hundreds-of-thousands/#.VovX2jZluRs.

pg. 7: Thoreau, Henry D. *Walden*. Princeton, NJ: Princeton University Press, 2004, p. 328.

CHAPTER ONE

pg. 14: Harding, Walter. *The Days of Henry Thoreau: A Biography*. (New York: Dover Publications, 1982), p. 8.

pg. 14: Harding, Walter. *The Days of Henry Thoreau: A Biography*, p. 9.

pg. 15: Harding, Walter. *The Days of Henry Thoreau: A Biography*, p. 14.

pg. 19: Richardson, Robert D., Jr. *Henry David Thoreau: A Life of the Mind*. (Berkeley, CA: University of California Press, 1986), p. 9.

pg. 19: Harding, Walter. *The Days of Henry Thoreau: A Biography*. p. 32.

pg. 20: Richardson, Robert D., Jr. *Henry David Thoreau: A Life of the Mind*, p. 10.

pgs. 21-22: Harding, Walter. T*he Days of Henry Thoreau: A Biography*, p. 37.

pg. 24: Harding, Walter. *The Days of Henry Thoreau: A Biography*, pp. 42–42.

pg. 24: Harding, Walter. *The Days of Henry Thoreau: A Biography*, p. 42.

pg. 26: Richardson, Robert D., Jr. *Henry David Thoreau: A Life of the Mind*, p. 13.

pg. 26: Thoreau, Henry D. *Walden*. (Princeton, NJ: Princeton University Press, 2004), p. 99.

CHAPTER TWO

pg. 30: Harding, Walter. *The Days of Henry Thoreau: A Biography*, p. 50.

pg. 30: *Ibid.*

pg. 33: Harding, Walter. *The Days of Henry Thoreau: A Biography*, p. 53.

pg. 34: Harding, Walter. *The Days of Henry Thoreau: A Biography*, p. 54.

pg. 34: Emerson, Ralph Waldo. *Nature and Selected Essays*. (New York: Penguin Books, 2003), p. 35.

pg. 41: Harding, Walter. *The Days of Henry Thoreau: A Biography*, p. 64.

pg. 42: Thoreau, Henry D. Ed. Damion Searls. *The Journal: 1837–1861*. (New York: New York Review of Books, 2009), p. 3.

pg. 42: Harding, Walter. *The Days of Henry Thoreau: A Biography*, p. 66.

pgs. 44-45: Richardson, Robert D., Jr. *Henry David Thoreau: A Life of the Mind*, 1986, p. 38.

pg. 45: Richardson, Robert D., Jr. *Henry David Thoreau: A Life of the Mind*, p. 42.

pg. 45: Richardson, Robert D., Jr. *Henry David Thoreau: A Life of the Mind*, p. 42.

pg. 45: Richardson, Robert D., Jr. *Henry David Thoreau: A Life of the Mind*, p. 41.

pg. 47: Harding, Walter. *The Days of Henry Thoreau: A Biography*, p. 117.

pg. 47: Harding, Walter. *The Days of Henry Thoreau: A Biography*, p. 118.

CHAPTER THREE

pgs. 49-50: Thoreau, Henry D. *Walden*, pp. 90–91.

pg. 50: Harding, Walter. *The Days of Henry Thoreau: A Biography*, p. 123.

pg. 50: Richardson, Robert D., Jr. *Henry David Thoreau: A Life of the Mind*, p. 113.

pg. 52: U.S. Bureau of the Census. "Population of the 100 Largest Urban Places: 1840." June 15, 1998, www.census.gov/population/www/documentation/twps0027/tab07.txt.

pg. 52: Richardson, Robert D., Jr. *Henry David Thoreau: A Life of the Mind*, p. 125.

pg. 52: Harding, Walter. *The Days of Henry Thoreau: A Biography*, p. 149.

pg. 53: Sullivan, Robert. T*he Thoreau You Don't Know: The Father of Nature Writers on the Importance of Cities, Finance, and Fooling Around.* (New York: Harper Perennial, 2009), p. 112.

pg. 54: Richardson, Robert D., Jr. *Henry David Thoreau: A Life of the Mind*, p. 149.

pg. 54: Richardson, Robert D., Jr. *Henry David Thoreau: A Life of the Mind*, p. 147.

pg. 60: Harding, Walter. *The Days of Henry Thoreau: A Biography*, p. 145.

pg. 60: Thoreau, Henry D. *Walden*, p. 31.

pg. 62: Brooks, Rebecca Beatrice. "Henry David Thoreau: The Woods Burner." History of massachusetts.org, http://historyofmassachusetts.org/henry-david-thoreau-woods-burner.

pg.62: *Ibid.*

pg. 63: Thoreau, Henry D. *Walden*, p. 69.

pg. 64: Richardson, Robert D., Jr. *Henry David Thoreau: A Life of the Mind*, p. 166.

pg. 64: Thoreau, Henry D. *Walden*, p. 8.

pg. 66: Thoreau, Henry D. *Walden*, p. 5.

pg. 66-67: Thoreau, Henry D. *Walden*, pp. 317–318.

pg. 67: Thoreau, Henry D. *Walden*, pp. 96–97.

CHAPTER FOUR

pg. 70: Harding, Walter. *The Days of Henry Thoreau: A Biography*, p. 200.

pg. 70: Harding, Walter. *The Days of Henry Thoreau: A Biography*, p. 201.

pg. 73: VandeCreek, Drew. "Origins." *Lincoln/Net*. Northern Illinois University Libraries. lincoln.lib.niu.edu/mexicanamerican/origins.

pg. 77: Thoreau, Henry D. "A Plea for Captain John Brown by Henry David Thoreau; October 30, 1859," avalon.law.yale. edu/19th_century/thoreau_001.asp.

pg. 79: Harding, Walter. *The Days of Henry Thoreau: A Biography*, p. 204.

pg. 79: Harding, Walter. *The Days of Henry Thoreau: A Biography*, p. 205.

pg. 79: *Ibid.*

pgs. 79-80: *Ibid.*

pg. 81: Young, Ralph F. *Dissent in America: 400 Years of Speeches, Sermons, Arguments, Articles, Letters, and Songs That Made a Difference.* (New York: Pearson Education, Inc., 2008), p. 127.

pg. 82: *Ibid.*

pgs. 82-83: *Ibid.*

pg. 83: Young, Ralph F. *Dissent in America: 400 Years of Speeches, Sermons, Arguments, Articles, Letters, and Songs That Made a Difference*, p. 128.

pgs. 83-84: Young, Ralph F. *Dissent in America: 400 Years of Speeches, Sermons, Arguments, Articles, Letters, and Songs That Made a Difference*, p. 135.

pg. 85: Sullivan, Robert. *The Thoreau You Don't Know: The Father of Nature Writers on the Importance of Cities, Finance, and Fooling Around*, p. 195.

CHAPTER FIVE

pg. 88: Harding, Walter. *The Days of Henry Thoreau: A Biography*, p. 245.

pg. 89: Harding, Walter. *The Days of Henry Thoreau: A Biography*, p. 254.

pg. 89: Sullivan, Robert. *The Thoreau You Don't Know: The Father of Nature Writers on the Importance of Cities, Finance, and Fooling Around*, p. 227.

pg. 90: Sullivan, Robert. *The Thoreau You Don't Know: The Father of Nature Writers on the Importance of Cities, Finance, and Fooling Around*, p. 193.

pg. 90: Sullivan, Robert. *The Thoreau You Don't Know: The Father of Nature Writers on the Importance of Cities, Finance, and Fooling Around*, p. 194.

pg. 91: Sullivan, Robert. *The Thoreau You Don't Know: The Father of Nature Writers on the Importance of Cities, Finance, and Fooling Around*, pp. 241–42.

pg. 94: Sullivan, Robert. *The Thoreau You Don't Know: The Father of Nature Writers on the Importance of Cities, Finance, and Fooling Around*, p. 239.

pg. 95: Sullivan, Robert. *The Thoreau You Don't Know: The Father of Nature Writers on the Importance of Cities, Finance, and Fooling Around*, p. 233.

pgs. 96-97: Sullivan, Robert. *The Thoreau You Don't Know: The Father of Nature Writers on the Importance of Cities, Finance, and Fooling Around*, p. 248.

CHAPTER SIX

pg. 100: Harding, Walter. *The Days of Henry Thoreau: A Biography*, p. 452.

pg. 100: Harding, Walter. *The Days of Henry Thoreau: A Biography*, p. 454.

pg. 100-101: Harding, Walter. *The Days of Henry Thoreau: A Biography.*, p. 457.

pg. 101: Harding, Walter. *The Days of Henry Thoreau: A Biography*, p. 461.

pg. 101: Harding, Walter. *The Days of Henry Thoreau: A Biography*, p. 466.

pg. 104: King, Martin Luther, Jr. "Letter from a Birmingham Jail." African Studies Center, University of Pennsylvania, www.africa. upenn.edu/Articles_Gen/Letter_Birmingham.html.

pg. 104: Sullivan, Robert. *The Thoreau You Don't Know: The Father of Nature Writers on the Importance of Cities, Finance, and Fooling Around*, p. 229.

FURTHER INFORMATION

BOOKS

Emerson, Ralph Waldo. *Nature and Selected Essays*. New York: Penguin Books, 2003.

Harding, Walter. *The Days of Henry Thoreau: A Biography*. 2nd ed, New York: Dover Publications, 2011.

Mooney, Edward F. *Excursions with Thoreau: Philosophy, Poetry, Religion*. London: Bloomsbury Academic, 2015.

Sullivan, Robert. *The Thoreau You Don't Know: The Father of Nature Writers on the Importance of Cities, Finance, and Fooling Around*. Reprint edition. New York: Harper Perennial, 2011.

Thoreau, Henry D. *I to Myself: An Annotated Selection from the Journal of Henry D. Thoreau*, edited by Jeffrey S. Cramer. New Haven: Yale University Press, 2012.

———. *Walden and Civil Disobedience*. New York: Signet, 2012.

WEBSITES

American Transcendentalism Web

transcendentalism-legacy.tamu.edu/authors/index.html

Texas A&M University hosts this exhaustive database on the roots, writings, and figures of the American Transcendentalist movement. In addition to articles introducing Transcendentalism and exploring some of the movement's major tenets, this website also features biographies on Ralph Waldo Emerson and Henry David Thoreau.

The Thoreau Reader

thoreau.eserver.org

Explore Thoreau's published books and essays for free with "The Thoreau Reader." In addition to accurate web reproductions of the texts themselves, this website features photos, histories, and criticisms of each of the works.

The Thoreau Society

www.thoreausociety.org

As part of its mission to preserve Thoreau's legacy and to challenge people to live deliberately as Thoreau did, the Thoreau Society hosts this excellent resource on all things Thoreau, from his life and travels to modern-day events and conferences.

The Walden Woods Project

www.walden.org/thoreau

The Walden Woods Project, a nonprofit organization with the mission of preserving Thoreau's literary accomplishments as well as Walden Pond itself, hosts this expansive resource on Thoreau's life. Here you will find articles on a range of topics, including Thoreau as a writer, Thoreau's reputation as a political and environmental activist, and many more.

The Writings of Henry D. Thoreau
thoreau.library.ucsb.edu

The University of California at Santa Barbara hosts this scholarly source on all of Thoreau's writings. In addition to links to his published books and essays, this site also features transcriptions of Thoreau's journals and correspondence, as well as an interactive scan of his handwriting.

MUSEUMS AND STATE RESERVATIONS

Concord Museum
www.concordmuseum.org/henry-david-thoreau-collection.php

53 Cambridge Turnpike
Concord, MA 01742

Walden Pond State Reservation
www.mass.gov/eea/agencies/dcr/massparks/region-north/walden-pond-state-reservation.html

915 Walden St.
Concord, MA 01742

BIBLIOGRAPHY

400 Years of Speeches, Sermons, Arguments, Articles, Letters, and Songs That Made a Difference. New York: Pearson Education, Inc., 2008.

Brooks, Rebecca Beatrice. "Henry David Thoreau: The Woods Burner." History of Massachusetts, August 14, 2012. Accessed December 26, 2015 (historyofmassachusetts.org/henry-david-thoreau-woods-burner).

Emerson, Ralph Waldo. *Nature and Selected Essays.* New York: Penguin Books, 2003.

Frederick, Michael J. "Transcendental Ethos: A Study of Thoreau's Social Philosophy and Its Consistency in Relation to Antebellum Reform," 1998. Accessed December 26, 2015 (thoreau.eserver.org/mjf/MJF1.html).

Harding, Walter. *The Days of Henry Thoreau: A Biography.* New York: Dover Publications, 1982.

Harvard University. "Josiah Quincy." Accessed December 26, 2015 (www.harvard.edu/about-harvard/harvard-glance/history-presidency/josiah-quincy).

InvestorPlace. "Report: Average American is $225,238 in Debt." Accessed January 5, 2016 (investorplace.com/2013/09/report-average-american-in-debt-hundreds-of-thousands/#.VovX2jZluRs).

Kays, Thomas A. "When Cross Pistareens Cut Their Way Through the Tobacco Colonies." *The Colonial Newsletter*. April 2001. Accessed December 26, 2015 (numismatics.org/wikiuploads/CNL/Pistareens.pdf).

King, Martin Luther Jr. "Letter from a Birmingham Jail." African Studies Center, University of Pennsylvania. Accessed December 26, 2015 (www.africa.upenn.edu/Articles_Gen/Letter_Birmingham.html).

"The Raid on Harpers Ferry." PBS.org. Accessed December 26, 2015 (www.pbs.org/wgbh/aia/part4/4p2940.html).

Richardson, Robert D. Jr. *Henry David Thoreau: A Life of the Mind*. Berkeley, CA: University of California Press, 1986.

Sullivan, Robert. *The Thoreau You Don't Know: The Father of Nature Writers on the Importance of Cities, Finance, and Fooling Around*. New York: Harper Perennial, 2009.

Thoreau, Henry D. "A Plea for Captain John Brown by Henry David Thoreau; October 30, 1859." Accessed December 26, 2015 (avalon.law.yale.edu/19th_century/thoreau_001.asp).

———. *The Journal: 1837–1861*. Edited by Damion Searls. New York: New York Review of Books, 2009.

———. *Walden and Resistance to Civil Government*. Edited by William Rossi. New York: W. F. Norton & Company, Inc., 1992.

———. *Walden*. Princeton, NJ: Princeton University Press, 2004.

The Walden Woods Project. "About Thoreau: A Brief Chronology." Accessed December 26, 2015 (www.walden.org/Library/About_Thoreau's_Life_and_Writings:_The_Research_Collections/A_Brief_Chronology).

Weiner, Gary, ed. *The Environment in Henry David Thoreau's* Walden. Michigan: Greenhaven Press, 2010.

U.S. Bureau of the Census. "Median and Average Square Feet of Floor Area in New Single-Family Houses Completed by Location." Accessed December 26, 2015 (www.census.gov/const/C25Ann/sftotalmedavgsqft.pdf).

———. "Population of the 100 Largest Urban Places: 1840." June 15, 1998. Accessed December 26, 2015 (www.census.gov/population/www/documentation/twps0027/tab07.txt).

VandeCreek, Drew. "Origins." *Lincoln/Net*. Northern Illinois University Libraries. Accessed December 26, 2015 (lincoln.lib.niu.edu/mexicanamerican/origins).

Young, Ralph F. *Dissent in America: The Voices That Shaped a Nation.*

INDEX

Page numbers in **boldface** are illustrations. Entries in **boldface** are glossary terms.

A Week on the Concord and Merrimack Rivers, 60–61, 66, 81, 87–90
abolitionism, 74, **78**, 79
abolitionists, 74, 76
apocryphal, 80
arson, 79

cabin, 7, 49–50, 54–55, **56**, **59**, 63, 66, 69, 79, 87
    furniture, 57
    supplies, 58
Cape Cod, 91, 94–95
capitulate, 79
christened, 14, 34, 54
"Civil Disobedience", 81, 85, 103
classics, 20, 44
coffin ship, **92–93**, 94
commonplace book, 26, **27**, 40
Concord Academy, 14, 18, **43**, 44, 46

Concord, MA, 7, 9–16, **10–11**, 26, 34, 37–38, 39–40, 42, 49–55, 60, 62, 69–70, 75–76, 79–80, 88, 90, 96, 100, 104
conflagration, 62
conscience, 7, 35, 38, 69, 75, 79, 81–85
cord, 12, 18
corporal punishment, 31, **32**, 44
credit, 33, 35
creditor, 33, 35, 66
crotchety, 81
culling, 35

democratic republic, 82
Dunkin Rebellion, 24

effigy, 24
Emerson, Ralph Waldo, 26, 30, 34–35, **36**, 37–38, 40–42, 45–47, 51, 53–55, 79–80, 84, 88, 96, 101
Emerson, William, 51, 53
Enlightenment, 38
environmental, 6, 62, 102–103
exorbitant, 14

farming industry, 10–12
flop, 88

Gandhi, 103–104

Harvard, 7, 18–24, **19**, 26–27, 29, 31, 37–38, 40–41, 90
    curriculum, 20
Hawthorne, Nathaniel, 84, 87–88, 101
homogenous, 12

individuality, 34, 38, 46–47

King, Martin Luther, Jr., 103–104

levy, 70
Locke, John, 38
lyceum movement, 37

malaise, 23
manifest destiny, 71, 94
manufacturing, 12, 17, 73, 89
Mexican-American War, 71, **72**, 74

naturalist, 69
Nature, 26, 34, 40
New York City, 50–51, **51**, 53–54

"On Resistance to Civil Government," 76, 79, 81–82, 84, 103

partisan, 74
peaceful resistance, 103
pencils, 12, 16, 17, 18, 53, 89, 97
philosophy, 30, 37–39, 44–45, 75
pistareen, 80
plumbago, 16
Polk, President James K., 73
prison, **68**, 69–70, 79–80, 85
prototypical, 30

Quincy, Josiah, 19–20, 22–24, **25**, 26, 35, 40

Revolutionary War, 13, **13**, 52
Romanticism, 37

slurry, 57
supplant, 52
surveying, 96–97, **97**, 99

tabula rasa, 38
teamster, 12
tetanus, 50
Thoreau, Cynthia, 14–15
Thoreau, John (brother), 18–19, 31, 44, 49–50, 54

Thoreau, John (father), 14–16,
    18, 40
Transcendentalism, 38, 96
tuberculosis, 23, 29, 35, 51, 99

Unitarianism, 35
unleavened, 60

Walden Pond, 15, 29, 39, **48**,
    49–50, 54–55, 58, 60, 69, 79,
    81, 87
Walden: or, Life in the Woods,
    7, 26, 49, 60, **61**, 62–63, 67,
    81, 87–90, 95, 97, 101
Wheeler, Charles Stearns, 29

ABOUT THE AUTHOR

Andrew Coddington has a degree in creative writing from Canisius College. He has written several books for Cavendish Square, including *Thomas Jefferson: Architect of the Declaration of Independence* in the Great American Thinkers series. He lives in Lancaster, New York, with his fiancée and dog.